YOU SHOULD HAVE
BEEN HERE LAST WEEK

&

Sharp Cuttings
from a Garden Writer

YOU SHOULD HAVE
BEEN HERE LAST WEEK

⤙

Sharp Cuttings
from a Garden Writer

Tim Richardson

PIMPERNEL
PRESS LTD
www.pimpernelpress.com

This book is dedicated to all the editors
who have ever commissioned me to write.*

Pimpernel Press Limited
www.pimpernelpress.com

YOU SHOULD HAVE BEEN HERE LAST WEEK
Sharp Cuttings from a Garden Writer

First published by Pimpernel Press Limited in 2016
This paperback edition first published by Pimpernel Press Limited
in 2018

Designed by Anne Wilson
Typeset in Minion

ISBN 978-1-910258-86-6
Printed and bound by CPI

2 4 6 8 9 7 5 3 1

COVER IMAGE
Shutterstock © Natalia Kudryavtseva

* You can contact me via the usual channels.

CONTENTS

INTRODUCTION

'YOU SHOULD HAVE BEEN HERE LAST WEEK.' That's what people always say to garden writers. Gardeners love telling you about that beautiful flowering shrub . . . which died last year. Or the magnificent display of blossom . . . which you have just missed. It transpires that failure is one of gardening's greatest attractions, especially for the British, who love talking about what has been lost or is missing even while surrounded by manifest success. This often amounts to passive-assertive boasting par excellence. And in the case of gardening it is often not failure at all, because most deaths in the garden can be attributed to that most natural of natural causes, the weather, while change is irrevocably bound up with the passage of the seasons.

But trumpeting our own powerlessness is a wonderful get-out clause when it comes to taking responsibility for either success or failure. The practice of garden-making therefore emerges as more elegiac in tone than celebratory. How paradoxical, given horticulture's ostensible preoccupation with the nurturing of new life. But the garden is a work of art which is a process, not a product, and that process includes death and decay.

The question I am most commonly asked, usually with more than a hint of incredulity, is: 'So how did you get interested in gardens?' I suppose I don't come across as a 'gardeny' sort of a person. Should I take this as a compliment? The articles gathered in this book reflect the fact that my preferred subject is not horticulture but garden culture. The invisible. So if an editor requests 800 words on the cultivation of sweet peas, then I have to decline. But if they were to ask me about the symbolic properties of sweet peas, or their place in the history of the herbaceous border – then I could perhaps help. Sometimes I joke that I operate at the extreme-pretentious end of garden writing.

This joke arises in part because, unlikely as it may sound, my first conscious critical engagement with gardens stemmed from an interest in art and poetry; it had nothing whatever to do with the joy of growing plants, and not much to do with an incipient interest in nature. It was the beauty of the moment and the power of place that ensnared me.

I went to Oxford to read English Literature with an idea that I might afterwards go on to do a post-graduate degree in art history, perhaps leading on to a curatorial job in a museum or gallery. I had studied art history at school, even though it was not on the curriculum, teaching myself and creating structure by giving mini-lectures to other sixth-formers on subjects such as Palladio's villas or the paintings of the Northern Renaissance. One of the topics I pursued was a study of the street furniture (benches, litter bins, lamps and so on) of my local town of Reading. A bit weird, I know. Aged seventeen, I had no idea there was something called landscape architecture, but I could see that such 'incidentals' were of aesthetic importance in an environment of little architectural merit. Independent study became my modus operandi, which is probably one of the reasons why I was attracted to the subject of gardens and garden history –relatively uncharted waters in academia. I like the way the garden can encapsulate interests in architecture, literature, pictorial composition, colour theory, natural forms, spatial design, ecology, cookery and the engineering of atmosphere.

By the age of eighteen I had visited, with my family, a large number of 'stately homes', plus nearly all the cathedrals in England and most of the Anglo-Saxon churches. I see now that gardens were also an important component of these trips, especially if we were accompanied by my grandfather. He and his two brothers had been professional gardeners at estates in Norfolk and Surrey, where my great-grandfather was head gardener. They had lived in the gardener's cottage at the end of the drive, where they received furniture, magazines and other paraphernalia from the 'big house'. I still have some of these hand-me-down heirlooms. My grandparents apparently first encountered each other on the back stairs, when Fred, the under-gardener, reportedly uttered to Lottie, the new junior housemaid, the immortal line: 'Would you like me to carry your coal-bucket?' Very Downton Abbey. A family background in domestic service means I have been comfortable writing about country houses.

Later – in a typical mid-twentieth-century demographic shift – my grandfather moved to Slough and became an electrical engineer at a power station. But gardens and vegetables remained major interests, and country ways a habit – I was told my grandad would take in a cabbage or cauliflower to work and boil it whole as his 'packed lunch'. At family lunches the quality of the vegetables and fruit, and their specific varieties, was always a topic of conversation. From an early age I was thus accustomed to hearing gardens discussed with a certain seriousness, and seeing them appraised on visits, too. I was the child who was taken to Alton Towers not to go on the theme-park rides but to tour the Victorian glasshouses.

I suppose all this must have had an influence on me.

By the mid-1980s, when I arrived at university, installation art was all the rage in the galleries. It had been around for some time, of course, but had only recently percolated through to the mainstream. At this period I began to visit eighteenth-century landscape gardens, chiefly because my poetic interests encompassed writers such as Alexander Pope, Thomas Gray and Johann Wolfgang von Goethe, all of whom looked upon gardens as a legitimate artistic genre. I had an epiphany at Studley Royal, in Yorkshire, where I suddenly realized that these landscape gardens, despite their popularity with the blue-rinse brigade, were nothing less than gigantic, ever-changing, walk-through art installations, replete with subtle meanings. Gallery-based work and even most land art suddenly seemed shallow and paltry in comparison. From there, it was not difficult to perceive flower borders as a form of 'painting with living pencils', as one eighteenth-century gardener put it, which opened up the world of twentieth-century herbaceous gardening.

At this time it was highly unusual for a young person to pursue an interest in gardens, and I recall being laughed at openly at parties if I mentioned it. So I rarely did. Architecture was, and remains, intellectually palatable, while gardens have never managed to clamber up to the High Table of academia (unless heavily disguised). There was, unaccountably, a sub-question about garden history in my Finals exams: this led several friends to scoff at the very idea – and to my shame I scoffed along with them. It seems I had a dirty little secret.

To my amazement I was invited to undertake a PhD on the poetry of Robert Browning – but I did not seriously consider it. After a very brief career as an actor and comedian (I co-starred in a Radio 4 comedy show at this time), which alternated with miserable periods of 'temping', I aimed for the publishing industry. I preferred words to performance – and anyway writing is a kind of performance (at least for me it is). I did not have it in mind to be a garden specialist at this time but I got a job working for eighteen months as freelance researcher, writer and finally editor of the biographical section on a new four-volume *RHS Dictionary of Horticulture*. This was its own kind of postgraduate qualification, based as it was in the libraries at Kew, the RHS and the Linnean Society, where I was looking into the 'lives' of celebrated gardeners, landscape designers, botanists and horticultural writers.

Neither had I ever imagined being a journalist, but I found myself learning my trade as a sub-editor on the *Antiques Roadshow Magazine*, simply because one of the publishers I wrote to on spec at this time was producing it on the side. I loved sub-editing because one must handle words almost as physical objects, honing sentences and articles into shape as delicately as possible. I still maintain that while anyone can be a writer of sorts, only someone with a deep affinity with words can edit properly. Poetic craft is more reminiscent, to me, of sub-editing than 'writing' (my first volume of poetry was published in 2015 – the result of an open competition). At Oxford I had given myself the task of examining Milton's use of punctuation, with a special emphasis on the semi-colon. I was interested in the mechanics of poetry, how it can elicit certain specific emotions in the reader. I have used the same kind of technique with my analyses of planting design and spatial organization in landscapes: anatomizing the design by taking it apart and construing its effects on those who experience it.

Editorial experience helped land me a job as a sub-editor on *Country Life* magazine. At my interview the editor asked me if I could ride. I answered yes, truthfully enough, though it was some years since I had been on a horse and even then hacking around the lanes on a farmer's nag was not exactly riding to hounds. At *Country Life* I gravitated towards the gardens pages from the start, but it is a large weekly magazine with a small staff and over my eight-year stint I was in addition books editor, exhibitions editor, property editor, motoring editor, news editor, sports editor and performing arts editor. In fact I am still a theatre critic for *Country Life*. At one point I remember being faced with a clear fork in the road: do I specialize in art, or in gardens? I chose the latter, and ended up as *Country Life*'s gardens editor.

I was not long in that post, however, because I had conceived of an idea for a new gardens magazine for a new generation, which after a fraught period of development was launched in 1999. *New Eden* lasted barely eighteen months – despite healthy sales and industry awards for its innovative design. It was closed along with several other magazines when the parent company failed to float on the stock market and was sold on to venture capitalists. At least people have held on to it – quite often when I visit design offices around the world, copies of *New Eden* are taken down from the shelves.

The magazine's closure was traumatic: *New Eden* had been 'my baby' and I had relinquished a good job at *Country Life*. But by this time I had a real baby, and the opportunity to pursue an independent career as a journalist and author. The editor of *Wallpaper** invited me to become (freelance) landscape editor at the magazine, and I became a regular contributor to the *Daily Telegraph*, where I now write a column under the sobriquet 'The Medlar'. *Gardens Illustrated* also became a regular outlet for my work, as did *House & Garden* and *English Garden*. In 2004 I was hired as a polemical and controversial columnist at the *Garden Design Journal* (*GDJ*), an opportunity I relished until, after a decade's contributions, I was dismissed via email for being (guess what?) too polemical and controversial (see pages 126 and 146). *GDJ* is a trade magazine, so its circulation was relatively small – but those columns nevertheless elicited more positive reaction from readers than anything else I have produced.

The closure of *New Eden* also meant that I was able to concentrate on my first book project, *The Garden Book*. Thirteen more books were to follow, the most noteworthy being *The Arcadian Friends: Inventing the English Landscape Garden* (2006), which proposes a political impulse for the creation of eighteenth-century landscape gardens; *Avant Gardeners* (2007), a celebration and definition of contemporary landscape conceptualism; and *The New English Garden* (2013), containing a narrative of the naturalistic turn in planting design over the past two decades.

The thrust of my career as an author has been two-pronged. On one hand I am a garden historian specializing in the early eighteenth-century landscape garden and on twentieth-century garden style in England, as well as diverse international topics (the gardens of ancient Korea are a preoccupation currently). On the other I have produced a number of books about trends in international landscape architecture and contemporary naturalistic planting design across Europe and beyond. To me it seems strange that so few of my colleagues in these two worlds – garden history and contemporary landscape criticism – seem willing to cross over into each other's territory.

Journalistic work is more varied and spontaneous, and provides a useful counterpoint to long-term book projects. It used to be that the impact of journalism was fleeting (the proverbial 'chip paper'), but one of the benefits of the Internet is that many articles are nowadays available online, and for an indefinite period. On my good days I feel like an independent scholar; on my less good days I feel like a hack journalist. Clearly I generally operate somewhere between these two poles. Rule number one is that I never write about gardens I have not personally visited (editors sometimes ask you to write an article, or even entire books, 'to the pictures'). My critical freedom is also jealously guarded: I do not join judging committees, selection panels or prize juries. This is to ensure that I can remain entirely independent as a critic. As for books, I no longer embark on projects which I want to write – I now have to feel I *need* to write them. The only serious frustration I encounter is when my work is poorly edited or rewritten, then sent to press without consultation – though this is mercifully rare.

My darkest secret is that I do quite like gardening, and have turned my north London garden into a kind of 'home allotment' fringed with flowering shrubs and choice perennials. In fact for about fourteen years now I have been having a passionate affair with the alluring Constance Spry in my back garden. 'Constance Spry' in inverted commas, that is – a 'shrub rose of arching habit with rounded, fully double, myrrh-scented pink flowers'. She is much more beautiful than that description implies, and more beguiling, even, than her picture on the Internet. But I shan't be writing about her any time soon.

The main selection criterion for the articles in this volume is that they should be enjoyable to read. Lengthy pieces, including my articles on historic gardens for *Country Life* and on art for *Apollo*, have been excluded. Barring a few last-minute substitutions, I have left the choice to my editor, on the principle that writers are not usually the best judges of their own work. As the great Dr Samuel Johnson once advised, 'Read over your compositions, and where ever you meet with a passage which you think is particularly fine, strike it out.' In this spirit I do hope you might meet with one or two things in this collection that you feel a sudden urge to 'strike out'.

Tim Richardson,
London, July 2016

TRENTHAM
FEBRUARY 2004

I HAVE SEEN THE FUTURE of garden design and it contains monkeys.

The revelation occurred at the press launch for the all-new Trentham Gardens in Staffordshire. Only three journalists turned up – two locals and one freelance (me) – at the buffet-lunch reception in a large marquee. But with a budget of £100 million and a heavyweight design team of Tom Stuart-Smith, Piet Oudolf and Dominic Cole of Land Use Consultants, the project surely requires our attention.

The monkeys came in to play early on. (Not literally.) An evangelical spokesman for St Modwen, the property company which is funding the work, described how the new Trentham will have something for everyone from tots to grannies: off-road motorsports in an old quarry, fine dining in the riverside restaurant, shops galore, a winery and – yes – a monkey sanctuary.

But what about the garden? The Italianate parterres at Trentham – laid out in the 1830s by Charles Barry in the shadow of one of his most successful houses – enjoy perhaps the most evocative setting of any formal garden in England, with long views across a mile of tranquil, tree-fringed lake. The place was new to me, and I was stunned. But the house was dismantled a century ago, and the garden has been neglected for some twenty years. The parterres are grassed-over, the yews are old and bulbous, the stonework is crumbling.

It seems that private investment has come to the rescue at Trentham, and there is no doubt that a first-class gardens team has been hired. But there is a price, of course. There is no public money going into this scheme, and the upfront plan is that all of it will be paid for through the leisure amenities in the wider estate (including those monkeys); a crafts retail village at the garden entrance; and a five-star hotel 'in the style of Barry' (probably a Marriott or similar) to be erected on the site of the house.

Now I am not saying this is necessarily a bad thing. If the Lottery (which only funds restoration schemes) had got its hands on Trentham, we would be faced with yet more unfettered Victoriana: 10,000 red salvias in tapestry formation. And it is exciting to anticipate what Stuart-Smith and Oudolf might make in this space. But the new Trentham is not about the garden, or even about the house. It is about the Trentham brand.

Whether we welcome it or not, branding is a growing trend in large-scale gardens, which aim to be visitor attractions first and foremost, with various other diversifications and 'stories' coming into play. One could call it the Heliganization of the scene, with Alnwick, Groombridge, Leeds Castle and now even 'quieter' gardens such as Painshill and Hestercombe beginning to envision themselves in this way. It could all lead to some interesting new, non-heritage commissions for garden designers. But be aware: you may have to work with monkeys.

Garden Design Journal

Trentham's rejuvenation proved a triumph; it is now one of Britain's horticultural highlights. The hotel was never realized; the monkey sanctuary was.

NEW PERENNIALS
JUNE 2004
↔

OVER THE PAST FEW MONTHS I have looked at thousands (yes, really) of photographs of twentieth-century planting schemes. This onerous task – research for a book – has provided me with quite a different perspective on the gardens of today.

My conclusion is that in the context of the planting trends of the previous century, many of the celebrated horticultural gardens of the nineties and the noughties look like pumped-up, muscle-bound confections, packed to bursting with flourishing and diverse plant material arranged in a bewildering tapestry of colours and shapes. There is no doubt that the practice of horticulture has improved – most gardens of the fifties and sixties look paltry in comparison – but standards of control and artistry are another matter. Gertrude Jekyll's original plantings, seen in contemporary photographs, appear positively spare next to today's rococo effusions, yet many gardeners who create 'Arts and Crafts' borders today believe that they garden authentically in her spirit.

It seems that we are now witnessing the late, decadent or Mannerist phase of Arts and Crafts gardening: a period when theories of colour in the mixed border have become well established and gardens such as Hadspen House, Somerset, can concentrate on minute, almost scientific gradations of colours in combinations. A period when gardeners seem to vie with each other to produce as many scintillating or unusual plant combinations as possible (something achieved with success at Great Dixter, East Sussex, but few other places). A period when eco-awareness and the fashion for meadows and organic gardening has meant that a sense of wild abandon and limitless profusion is a leitmotif amid all of this. The result is a garden that appears to be on steroids, so full of 'wow factor' that the attentive visitor comes away feeling exhausted, confused and faintly nauseous.

But there is a way out. The New Perennials movement, with drifts of grasses and sculptural, late-flowering plants, is a genuinely refreshing alternative that also – crucially – seems to chime with the times. Perhaps its most liberating aspect is the abandonment of colour as a guiding principle. Yes, there are problems: can it work on a small scale? Is it over-hyped? But this look represents a lifeline from the downward spiral of twentieth-century pastiche Arts and Crafts. True believers include John Brookes, Christopher Bradley-Hole, Dan Pearson, Isabelle van Groeningen and Noel Kingsbury, as well as all those Dutchmen.

I used to think that New Perennials might turn out to be a flash in the pan – but not any more. I am converted. (Oh, and I'll have 600 *Miscanthus sinensis* 'Morning Light', please.)

Garden Design Journal

SISSINGHURST
JULY/AUGUST 2004
⊸

I WENT TO SISSINGHURST, KENT, recently and was appalled. It wasn't that it was badly gardened (it wasn't) and it wasn't because my National Trust carrot cake had a toenail in it (it didn't) – it was just that it felt like a con. Every day, coachloads of people turn up at Sissinghurst to experience Vita Sackville-West's garden, yet what they get bears no relation to the original in terms of content or atmosphere. In a nutshell, Sackville-West's Sissinghurst was a tumbledown garden where plants encroached from every side, whereas the National Trust's Sissinghurst is a manicured visitor attraction. It is a travesty of the original.

I am not blaming the NT or its gardeners for this: what has happened at Sissinghurst is symptomatic of our restoration-obsessed age, and can be seen at many gardens where the person who made them has died and the new custodians are trying to retain some of the same atmosphere. The day before, I visited East Lambrook Manor, in Somerset, to find new owners dedicated to resurrecting the garden in the style of Margery Fish. But why? Surely it is impossible? If we continue like this, we will end up with the horticultural equivalent of an art gallery full of fakes.

We have entered a post-makeover age (not that *that* matters to anyone except television execs), but perhaps we are in a post-restoration era, too. That was certainly the feeling I had at the end of a conference on 'restoration philosophy' at the Architectural Association in April.

Restoration works best in gardens which are not chiefly dependent on horticulture – the eighteenth-century landscape garden is a good example. In gardens which are all about a particular individual who worked there, and the complexities of his or her planting style and design, it is obvious that we are on a hiding to nothing. No one has ever managed to create a garden quite as Gertrude Jekyll did. Is it fair to ask today's gardeners to compromise their own creativity and spend their careers 'working in the spirit of' someone who is long dead?

Perhaps it is time for the NT and other custodians to consider giving today's leading gardeners and garden designers a chance. The Trust could invite them to take over at some of its properties, to live in the house and be given almost a free rein in the garden. This is in effect what happened at Tintinhull with Penelope Hobhouse (apparently to the NT's displeasure).

No sensitive designer would ever destroy what has gone before. The living garden would again be associated with a living person; visitor numbers would increase; and the garden would no longer be engaged in a policy that smacks of dishonesty or folly. At Sissinghurst, for example, wouldn't a real Dan Pearson be more exciting than a fake Vita? Perhaps it is time to say goodbye to the 'White Garden' – it is what Vita would have wanted, surely?

Garden Design Journal

In 2015 Dan Pearson was engaged as a design consultant at Sissinghurst, working with head gardener Troy Scott Smith on the re-Vita-lization of Sissinghurst (see pages 183–4).

EXISTENTIALIST GARDENING
FEBRUARY 2005
⌘

THIS DARK MONTH OF FEBRUARY has inspired the theme of existentialist gardening. It may sound a bit pretentious or highfalutin, but why not? If we want gardens to be considered on the same level as literature, or art, or music, or architecture, surely we should be able to discuss them in such terms? Anyway, it's a bit of fun, as they say.

The key to the idea of existentialist gardening is the experiential nature of the garden as an art form. Existentialism emphasizes all that is unique and particular about human experience, even if – especially if – it cannot be reconciled with the generalized truisms of human nature which we are taught, or scientifically derived ways of looking at the world that seem divorced from real experience. For the existentialist, the truth of the world is rather in life as it is lived, the 'lifeworld', ideally interpreted through the integrity of the individual and not through a filter of pre-existing ideas. This may be an impossibility in practice, but it is the effort that counts.

As we all know – but do not often elucidate – the garden, more than any other medium, represents the interface between mankind and nature, the point where we seek physically to emplace ourselves in the universe. This makes gardens profoundly distinct from the other art forms, because when we walk in a garden, the human body becomes central to the experience, subsumed in the place and even acting as a co-creator of it – since, on some level, our interactions will always alter the place for future visitors.

Without the transformative participation of the observer, any aesthetic moment is incomplete – yet gardens have this quality to a higher degree than any other art form.

So gardening chimes with existentialist philosophy because the psychic human experience, and the physical presence of the body itself, are seen as subsumed into the place.

Space – in the geometrical, Euclidean sense, or in the physical, Newtonian sense – is not in this view the organising principle of place; it is the indivisible mind and body that are. As the philosopher Martin Heidegger put it, 'When we speak of man and space, it sounds as though man stood on one side, space on the other. Yet space is not something that faces man. It is neither an external object nor an inner experience.'

Another philosopher who touched on this theme is Maurice Merleau-Ponty – Sartre's great rival – who returned repeatedly to the subject of Cézanne, noting the crucial distinction that he did not 'paint landscapes'; but he painted the landscapes of Provence. In other words, the visual component was not necessarily the painter's paramount concern in terms of his inspiration: 'What motivates the painter's movement can never be simply perspective or geometry or the laws governing colour . . . Motivating all the movements from which a picture gradually emerges there can be only one thing: the landscape in its totality and its absolute fullness.' This is also how garden and landscape designers operate.

It is surely only a matter of time before Homebase starts selling black polo necks and Gauloises cigarettes as everyday gardening accoutrements.

Garden Design Journal

SMALL GARDENS
APRIL 2005
↩

THE BASIC PROBLEM is that the small garden almost always looks dreadful. My garden looks dreadful. My neighbours' gardens look dreadful. All the small gardens shown on television look dreadful, as do nearly all of those illustrated in books. Most of the small gardens designed by garden designers look dreadful. The plants might be thriving, but in design terms the majority of the small gardens opened to the public for the National Gardens Scheme and others look dreadful, too. Ninety-five per cent of the gardens designed for shows – from the Royal Horticultural Society's Chelsea Flower Show down – look dreadful.

Now I realize I may not be making many friends among readers with this broad accusation of dreadfulness, but this situation must be seen in part as a reflection of the collective failure of the garden design profession through the twentieth century and beyond. There has been a failure to popularize a coherent design vocabulary for the small garden, despite valiant efforts by the likes of John Brookes and Margery Fish (at opposite ends of the ideological design spectrum).

Such a bleak conclusion must be larded with the caveat that the problem of how to design a small garden space is extremely difficult to resolve in theory as well as practice. I was looking through an obscure, late magazine article by Gertrude Jekyll the other day (in *Our Homes and Gardens*, April 1925), one of very few where she grappled with the needs of the small or suburban garden – and even she did not get it right. She seemed unable to conceive of the small garden as anything except a scaled-down rendition of one of her Surrey extravaganzas.

The problem is rooted in the fact that in the first half of the twentieth century, the design vocabulary for smaller gardens was based entirely on the Arts and Crafts inheritance of designers such as Mackay Hugh Baillie Scott and Charles Voysey. Decorative features which were suitable for medium-sized gardens were miniaturized and thereby made absurd in smaller spaces. Think of wishing wells and crazy paving, as well as the ubiquitous lawn, herbaceous border and line of standard roses. The situation has not changed much today, in that we are still encouraged – even by today's design books – to think of the garden as a repository for ornamental 'features' or other leisure and lifestyle accoutrements. All too often, a plethora of plants only adds to the confusion. Garden plans published in books and used as the basis for teaching tend to encourage this approach, whereas in reality, many of the best small gardens cannot be usefully described in plan form because everything really interesting is happening above ground level, as it were, or else is invisible.

This may sound rather obvious to designers, but I do not see this kind of focus translated into many real gardens, even those published in books and held up to us as exemplars. It is notable that the best designers and writers of the past century – people like Russell Page, Lanning Roper, Sylvia Crowe and Ralph Dutton

– spent a lot of time urging people to leave things out of their designs. The principle of subtraction is not necessarily a recipe for minimalism: a profuse cottage garden can work well on a small scale, so long as it retains its simple integrity and is not cluttered up with other ideas.

But the big problem remains: why do so many small gardens, even designed ones, look so dreadful?

Garden Design Journal

DREADFUL
MAY 2005
↝

'DREADFUL'. Several readers were prompted by my last contribution to question what it was, specifically, I meant by that word in relation to almost all small-garden design in this country, during the past century. So here goes.

By 'dreadful' I mean principally the error of trying to pack too much in to the space – whether that be ornamental or lifestyle 'features' which people think they want; a plethora of plant varieties; or simply too many ideas going on in the area available. Of course, the quality of materials is even more important in a smaller garden, where everything will be under closer scrutiny, and it is usually a mistake simply to miniaturize garden styles that have been admired elsewhere. But while the pitfalls of pastiche and the importance of detail are obviously issues for designers, I am not just talking about the quality of the paving and the expression on the gnomes' faces. The problem has lain with our psychological approach to small-space design.

There has been a strong temptation to succumb to the idea of a garden as a place that needs filling up with things. The drawn plan can encourage this tendency, since the onus is on occupying all those little gridded squares with material, instead of coming up with a basic idea or theme and letting it colonize the space conceptually, before it does physically. Russell Page enlarged upon this in *The Education of a Gardener* (1962): 'Tensions of a certain kind play a large and unsuspected part in composition. As with the interrelations of patches of colour in painting, so between the solid objects in a garden certain tensions or vibrations are established around an object and between one object and another across the intervening air.'

Page is delving into the realms of philosophy and sculpture here – Jean-Paul Sartre and Andy Goldsworthy are among those who have made similar points about the affective qualities of objects – but what he is saying has practical relevance to garden design: every object and every plant exudes its own meanings to the visitor. So it makes sense that the mind guiding the design makes sure that as far as possible each object is contributing to 'a single idea beautifully phrased' (Lutyens's words), and also that the number of objects, or sets of similar objects (such as plants), so employed is kept to a minimum.

Several twentieth-century commentators have made the same basic point about the dangers of over-elaboration in small gardens, many of which were created after all as backyards rather than as blank canvases for the creation of ornamental gardens. Richard Sudell in *Landscape Gardening* (1933) observed: 'We have had too much material, we have had many ideas. Our gardens suffer from a surfeit of good and indifferent things . . . We are thus involved in complexity, and this, in a nut-shell, is the reason for the need of careful design.' The inimitable Jason Hill in *The Contemplative Gardener* (1939) put it this way: 'The general practice of gardening is so steadily towards filling up and putting in that there is something almost unnatural in making empty spaces and leaving them bare.'

Nothing has changed. In fact, things have got worse. During the past few decades the point about reductionism has been made far less frequently, perhaps because most writers have been concerned with the minutiae of herbaceous planting design. In my experience, the best small gardens are those made by the owners over a period of time, while the worst are those which have been subjected to a 'design'. Good small gardens are not made by 'planning' or by finding 'design solutions' (phrases that occur all the time in the titles of garden design books) – they are made by a conceptual, psychological and emotional involvement with the space and the people who are to use it.

Garden Design Journal

GARDEN ORNAMENT
NOVEMBER 2005

Is GARDEN ORNAMENT the love that dare not speak its gnome? It is a taboo subject in garden design because tastes vary so widely. That's the polite way of putting it. Garden designers know that when a client mentions casually on the phone that they have just installed a 'lovely figurine' purchased at the Hampton Court Palace Flower Show, they might as well have admitted to detonating a medium-sized bomb in the garden.

I don't want to harp on about how awful most garden ornament for sale is. That is taken as a given. There is of course a good deal of excellent stuff out there, too, and every designer will have their favourites (and if you haven't seen it yet, the new Barbed gallery in Barnes, west London, is worth checking out: www.barbed.co.uk). But perhaps it is worth making a few observations about ornament, if only as a tool for dissuading clients from going 'arty' and placing a frog wearing a golden crown in the middle of the lawn.

The problem with 'decoration' or 'ornament' is that the very words imply superfluousness. William Morris enjoined us to allow only the beautiful and useful into our homes, and functionalist Modernists of the 1960s and 1970s spurned all decoration. But why does everything have to be useful? Surely there is a place for decorative objects in the eclectic contemporary garden?

Such artefacts seem to work best when conceived as part of a coherent total design, not simply plonked down in the space to make it appear pretty or arty. 'Twas ever thus. Here is James Ralph, writing of statuary in *A Critical Review of the Publick Buildings… in London* (1734): 'A statue … should, by its own nature, be suited to the place. To compleat an area, end a vista, adorn a fountain, or decorate a banquetting-house or alcove, is the just and natural use of statues: not to people a garden, and make a nuisance of what ought to be a beauty.'

Good contemporary use of ornament and painted decoration can be seen in the work of designers such as George Carter and Anthony Noel. They show that strong decorative statements will work if they are consistently extended through the garden. Classical objects – either reclaimed (old) or reconstituted (new) – can work well if they are allowed to dictate the feel of the whole garden; we learned that from Harold Peto. Similarly, modern sculpture must be allowed to exert its power over a whole garden, as Jellicoe proved with the Sutton Place relief and the owners of Antony House in Cornwall demonstrate with the complementary placement of a William Pye piece amid topiary.

The other alternative is to allow decorative objects to melt into the scene, to become part of the structure rather than stand-alone objects. Sissinghurst, which contains more decorative ornament than is sometimes remembered, is an object lesson in this, as is the Modernist use of large, gracefully aged terracotta urns as garden punctuation (see Mien Ruys, John Brookes and Peter Aldington).

Perhaps it all seems rather obvious. But go to any garden show and you can still see designers falling into the trap of incorporating too many decorative 'voices' in a single design. It makes for a cacophony of the styles, and earplugs will not help.

Garden Design Journal

HORTICULTURAL MONOMANIA
APRIL 2006

BRITAIN has been in the grip of a horticultural monomania for the past three-quarters of a century and that grip is as tight as ever. In this country, for the vast majority, plants still define gardens and gardens still define plants. This attitude resonates into the realm of professional garden design, where we still have a phantom division between those who plant and those who design gardens. I say phantom because there is no such thing as a garden-maker who can plant but not design, or a garden- maker who can design but not plant. But a large number of designers do see themselves as falling into one or other camp, and like to snipe at the other side. The reality is that every designer finds their own place on the sliding scale between the two extremes of (1) fanatical train spotter-type plantsperson and (2) pretentious design-obsessive with media glasses (see . . .). If this is the case, then 'Why oh why' – to be said in a whiny voice – 'Why can't we all just get along?'

The debate, if we can call it that, is really just a rehash of the hackneyed and bogus division between craft and art which has dogged domestic and 'female' creative pursuits for centuries. It is partly fuelled by caricatures created by both 'sides', which are themselves the result of palpable insecurities about respective skill-sets. (I can't believe I have just used the word 'skill-sets'; perhaps I should warn that in future columns I will be rolling out self-referenced outreach footprints to consolidate skill-set interfacing for garden designers. With maps, if you need to escape.) Designers like to say that plantspeople have no feeling for anything beyond the flower immediately in front of them (and whether it is rare or not), while horticulturists are constantly harping on about the lack of plant knowledge among trained designers today. (The latest salvo came from Sybille Kreutzberger, ex-Sissinghurst gardener, interviewed in *The Garden* last month.) We should have fewer designers and more gardeners, they say, as if the boom in garden design has something to do with successive governments' systematic dismantling of local authority parks departments.

I don't know if you have noticed this, but when I go abroad – particularly to the USA – the impression people have of the British garden scene is that it is stuck in this horticultural rut of herbaceous borders and country garden planting. It is a quaint 1950s and 1960s view of Britain, bracketed with the royal family, the Beatles, umbrellas and Earl Grey tea. In some ways we fully deserve this, and it does garner us a respect of sorts. But it really is not good enough. Few outside Britain seem to realize that many garden-makers here have moved on from the 1950s and Margery Fish cottage planting, away from the connoisseurial obsessions of an influential few plant 'gurus' and their acolytes in print, who bully the rest of us into believing that to garden well we must grow a wide range of plants. We need to jettison the horticultural baggage of the past and assert ourselves in new ways. We need to get to a place where a designer can say, 'I don't know that much about plants' without fear of vilification.

In short, the (gardening) gloves need to come off. Well, we don't need them on, do we? Because, as the 'gardeners' say, 'designers' never get their hands dirty anyway.

Garden Design Journal

PLANTS AND ARCHITECTURE
OCTOBER 2006

I SEEM TO HAVE DEVELOPED an irrational aversion to any description of plants being used to 'soften' architecture. When some unsuspecting garden designer uses this apparently innocent form of words, my eyes narrow and I find myself retorting slowly, in a low voice and with menacing deliberation: 'Now what, exactly, do you mean by "soften"?' It happened again the other week and the poor lady nearly choked on her vol-au-vent. What a strange reaction in me! 'Soften'

is such a gentle little word. Perhaps I have been hypnotized by Paul McKenna and it has become a 'trigger'? I can't remember being hypnotized. But then again, I wouldn't . . . Or perhaps it is all bound up with the realization that this commonplace idea among garden designers is symptomatic of a malaise in British garden design, whereby plants and 'hard materials' are seen as intractable opposing forces which must somehow be reconciled. Yes, that must be it.

It is all rather strange because Lutyens and Jekyll supposedly 'solved' this problem a century ago. But their rationale has been misunderstood. Rather than 'softening' or 'clothing' Lutyens's structure with plants, Jekyll – who hated ivy and other climbers on walls – actually bolstered the lines of the architecture by the use of sturdy plant groupings placed for structural emphasis, as well as for rhythmic and directive functions. That is a much harder effect to achieve than simply obscuring brick and stonework. It is true that in some instances it is right to use plants to cover ugly things, but such cases should be the exception that proves the rule.

British garden design is rightly praised for its generally high standard of plantsmanship, but there is a concomitantly low standard when it comes to the selection and deployment of stone, brick, wood and concrete. The Royal Horticultural Society regularly awards its 'coveted' medals to gardens where the design of the hard landscaping is poor. These gardens are often sponsored by stone manufacturers.

In the mainstream, too many designers seem to be turned on by plants first of all and direct 90 per cent of their creative energies to that end. While not necessarily a recipe for disaster, it can certainly be a shortcut to mediocrity. Even in consummate cottage gardens such as Margery Fish's East Lambrook Manor in Somerset, the network of paths, and the hard materials used, made an important contribution to the look of the garden. Bricks, slabs, pebbles and decorative features should be conceived – and genuinely conceived – in tandem with planting schemes and executed with the same level of discernment. Only then will the absurdity of constructing something only in order to 'soften' it become apparent.

Garden Design Journal

PERSONAL QUESTIONS
DECEMBER 2006

Two PERSONAL QUESTIONS seem to crop up when people learn of a professional interest in gardens. First: how did you get into gardening in the first place? (In my case, asked in a slightly incredulous tone.) Second: so what is your own garden like? (Even more incredulous.)

There are all kinds of answers to the first question, and it is easy enough to palm off the inquisitor with a stock response. The best answer from a commercially minded designer would probably be that you started gardening just as soon as your tiny eyes opened, grasping a baby-sized trowel as you cultivated mustard and cress for your fellow carpet-crawlers. The truth, of course, is that many people come to gardening when they are older, possibly wiser and certainly more reflective about the correlation between income and job satisfaction. My own answer is always 'eighteenth-century poetry', which is partially true and also, of course, amazingly pretentious – a deliberately unhorticultural response. Which leads us on to the next question.

People often expect garden designers (and writers) to have wonderful gardens which somehow epitomize their own signature style. When people ask what my own garden is like, my stock response is, 'A disgrace'. This answer is intended to be taken with a pinch of salt, because I actually like gardening, without making any great claims for my own skill. But I respond in this way on principle, because I am first of all a writer – no one asks architectural critics what their bricklaying is like, or art critics whether they can paint. I also do it to annoy certain other garden writers, who suspect I am a fraud because I have not won any horticultural prizes and do not live in the country. (The ploy can backfire, as it did for me on a Radio 4 consumer show a few years ago when the host – an American with an irony bypass – did not chuckle as I intended her to when I said my garden was a disgrace, but responded with, 'Well, that's not very inspiring for our listeners!')

It is the same for designers. Why should their own gardens be works of art? Why should they even need to have a garden? We all need a break. Some people make a showcase which is open to the public, and fair enough, but a designer's home plot might just as easily bear no resemblance to their professional work – as with Thomas Church's tiny San Francisco yard, for example, or the penthouse flat with only a balcony where Sir Geoffrey Jellicoe lived in later years. Vegetables can be a great relief after miles of mixed borders, and there might even be a perverse pleasure in letting one's own plot slightly run to seed (though that would of course be quite fashionable at the moment).

'So what's your own garden like?' The way this essentially impertinent question is posed, and the way designers feel they need to respond to it, is actually quite a useful barometer with regard to the status of garden design in this country. Many people still think of garden designers as jumped-up Percy Throwers – an idea reinforced by *Ground Force*, where Alan T. apparently evolved overnight from gumbooted gardener to style guru, cobbling together 'designs' out of miscellaneous stock features in an afternoon or two. Perhaps it is time to start asserting more strongly the fact that this is a design discipline, not just a hobby that turned into a job, and that one's own garden is in many ways an irrelevance.

Garden Design Journal

LOVE OF PLANTS
APRIL 2007
✧

MY DAILY BIKE COMMUTE across north London takes me right past two prisons, which keeps me on the straight and narrow, obviously. The other day, however, I was arrested just along from HMP Holloway.

Not 'arrested' in a criminological sense, but 'arrested' in the sense of stopped in my tracks at the sight of a large cherry tree which had just burst into fresh flower from its roadside position in front of a council block. ('Arrested' – good eh? Consummate wordsmithery from your humble scribe, resident punmeister, etc., etc. . . .)

Now this cherry was just a bog-standard street tree, but all the same I nearly fell off my bike at the sight of its nascent blossom. In fact, it made me cry – what was that about? It made me ponder anew the role of plants in gardens, and our relationship with them, as garden-makers.

The Modernist mantra is that plants and flowers should be considered as just another material in the garden, alongside bricks, stonework, water, wood and space itself. I have to confess that I have repeated this mantra myself on numerous occasions over the years. Design books recommend plants for their practical qualities above all, while in the realm of horticulture plants are appraised as 'good performers' or 'worthwhile subjects', to be given an Award of Garden Merit by the Royal Horticultral Society – as if functioning as cogs in a well-oiled garden machine. Even Gertrude Jekyll appraised plants in a 'scientific' way, in terms of their coloration (in print at least).

Can this be right? It does not seem to reflect our actual relationship with plants, which is emotional as much as anything else. In reality, no one who works with gardens takes a purely functionalist view of plants, whatever they might read or say. The emotive qualities of plants as a 'material' are unique, not just in the matter of the palette available to garden designers, but in the palettes available to designers or artists in any discipline. The only possible exception is the meaning of stone to sculptors (remembering Michelangelo's conviction that forms were trapped inside his blocks of Carrara marble and that he was liberating them rather than creating them through his carving).

My point is that we should not underestimate this emotional aspect of planting design at the planning stage, simply because it is impossible to illustrate with visual aids and is perhaps slightly embarrassing to 'fess up to. An affection for plants – both as species or varieties in a general sense, or as individual specimens in particular – is all part of the identity of the garden-maker.

And a meaningful, two-way relationship with certain plants is a core aspect of gardening. It might seem an obvious point, but it is curious that this is something which is hardly ever talked about by designers. Is it yet another form of love that dare not speak its name?

Garden Design Journal

MY WEEK
MAY 2007

To APSLEY HOUSE – not for a grand military dinner but as a parent accompanying my six-year-old son's class outing. I am the only male in sight, which is usually the way with these things. Each adult is assigned five children for the day, and although it is disconcerting to have some re-sealable plastic bags thrust into my hands when boarding the coach, because the child who suffers from travel sickness is in my group, there are no upsets.

Stranded on Hyde Park Corner's roundabout, Apsley House looks like one of those buildings in Blitz photos, left eerily standing alone amid the devastation. Inside, although there are outstanding works by Velazquez – implacable Pope Innocent X trumps anything Francis Bacon did to him – it is clear that the Duke of Wellington had not an iota of taste. No matter: he stuffed Boney.

We meet 'Hannah the housemaid', our guide and chaperone for the day. Among much else, we learn that in the pre-Dyson age old tea leaves would be sprinkled on the carpet as a way of attracting the dust before sweeping. In the treasure room I point out to the boys all the 'real' swords and the battle scenes painted on porcelain (well, I am the man of the group) and am just discoursing on the savage effectiveness of the kukri dagger when a decision is taken to usher us into the next room.

My group are given a chamberpot and have to guess what it is for. The answers range from porridge receptacle to flower vase to ice bucket. No one comes close to the dread truth: a chamberpot lifestyle is clearly beyond modern imaginings.

* * *

WAR LOOMS LARGE in this building – not so much a house as a memorial to a military career. A panorama of the Battle of Waterloo is discussed; the guide is admirably direct about the reality of battle. 'How many died in total on that day?' she enquires. The answers vary: '200? . . . 850? . . . 1,200? . . . 2,000?' The true figure is an estimated 45,000 men. 'How do you think the people back home felt when they heard the British had won and that their son or brother or father was coming home?' 'Happy,' the children answer in unison. One little girl puts her hand up. 'I think the people whose father or brother or son had died would feel sad,' she says.

The children are set to work copying a detail of the painting, and pencil problems soon arise. 'My dad always has a pencil sharpener in his pocket,' my son announces, adding: 'He's a real writer.' So I sharpen various pencils quietly until the class teacher approaches. 'Do you really carry a pencil sharpener with you all the time?' she asks. 'Yes,' I reply meekly. She looks at me with a mixture of pity and curiosity, before responsible-teacher mode kicks in: 'What are you doing with the shavings?' (There are no bins in Apsley House.) 'I'm putting them in a little bag,' I state pathetically. I begin to explain that I carry a pencil sharpener because I work in the British Library, where you can only use pencils, and that the bag is one of those I had been given earlier in case of travel sickness . . . but the damage has been done. I am Spod Daddy number one, with my pencil sharpener and my little bag of shavings. Serves me right for being bigged up by my son.

* * *

ANOTHER DAY, another trip, this time to the Eden Project, in not-quite deepest Cornwall. As a repeat visitor to Legoland, I am not going to be snobby about Eden. The crucial thing to realize about the place is that it is not really a garden at all: it is a crowd-pleasing visitor attraction. Chatsworth it ain't.

I cannot help my own prejudices, however, and to me the huge plasticky bubbles ('biomes') seem rather ugly and the other buildings an unholy mish-mash, though the place undoubtedly has an unforgettable extraterrestrial flavour. There is some lovely planting in the South African section with – warning: I am going to get a bit nerdy now– quite the best display of restionaceae grasses I have seen in this country.

The only really strange moment (and therefore the most memorable one) comes when I enter the rainforest biome. The sliding-door entrance is hard by the large indoor cafeteria, and thanks to a downward blast of cool air at the entrance/exit, the unmistakable smell of 'dinner' is wafted in for a distance of at least 50 metres. The aroma of this indeterminate stew catapults me straight back to school dinner queues, an intense but incongruous accompaniment to my experience of the flora of the equatorial jungle. Somehow I expect the scent of chocolate sponge with custard to arise by way of natural conclusion as I penetrate deeper into the jungle. But the smello-vision fades out . . .

. . . only to return again as I approach the exit. I must remember to temper my expectations accordingly when I get to visit the real rainforest.

Country Life

TOM STUART-SMITH
JULY 2007
✧

GARDEN DESIGNERS adopt a variety of attitudes to their own gardens. Some of them choose to create a kind of public showcase for their 'signature style', while others take the opportunity to make a garden quite out of professional character, or even eschew a garden entirely. Most often, perhaps, designers come to see their own private space as an opportunity to relax and experiment. That is precisely what Tom Stuart-Smith has been doing since 1987 in his own garden at Serge Hill, near Abbots Langley in Hertfordshire. Tom describes the garden as, 'unstable . . . here I can do all the things which I would never do elsewhere. It's a playground. I can make impulsive decisions, never plan, make mistakes, rootle around and generally not be too organized.' This garden is clearly a relief.

The first project here was the house, which was converted from a derelict barn complex on land adjacent to the farmhouse where Tom was brought up. The bucolic setting, on a hilltop just off a country lane, belies the notion that it is impossible to find countryside so close to London. Here, in a pocket of arable farmland, Tom has been able to create a magical and intimate garden that truly 'clothes' the house in the way he intends, so that a single domestic sensibility pervades the place as a whole, regardless of whether one is inside or out.

The first garden space one sees here is the sunken courtyard garden that prefaces the barn. This year Tom has been overseeing a complete overhaul of the space, reusing a Corten steel wall and long tank made for his Chelsea-winning 2006 show garden. Tom hopes that the addition of some elegant decked areas will make the courtyard seem more usable, since previously people have tended to skirt round it on the brick terrace above.

The garden proper begins as one steps through the double doors that open from the main living area of the barn. Tom's basic idea has been to unite the garden with its surroundings, to create a harmonious balance between nature and artifice. From a small terrace a straight vista speeds westwards over a lozenge of lawn flanked by a pair of short but deep borders, past more borders – this time dignified by a group of columnar yews and some low box hedges – and on to a tall clipped hornbeam hedge complex, pierced to allow for the vista to continue along a mown path through meadow beyond before dissolving into woodland.

The garden splits into three main spaces: this main vista and its borders; a larger and wilder section of garden to the south, made up of five irregular planting areas around a central hornbeam structure; and the high-hedged hornbeam area to the west and north – just lawn, no flower colour – which acts as a green palette cleanser. Beyond all that lies the meadow to the north, woodland to the south, and all around the gently undulating countryside, which is as much a part of the garden as anything else.

As Tom explains, this is not a garden with a beginning, a middle and an end, working as a sequential experience of contrasting spaces: it operates more as a tone poem, its moods and moments surging and receding but always unified by an all-pervading tone and rhythm. 'I never think of these spaces as rooms – I like everything to interconnect,' he explains. 'One overall story, with a series of subplots, not a series of episodes. I want the whole garden to be one malleable entity.' Tom's method of showing the garden seems to chime with this attitude: he immediately whisks me off round the garden, with no time to stop and stare. It transpires that the idea is to go round three or four times, and in different directions, to absorb the flavour of the place as a whole.

The main move in terms of planting is defined by Tom as 'a gradient of naturalness' between those areas nearest to and farthest from the house, while the hedged structures incidentally create a sense of rhythm and direction as well as surprise vistas out. This is an unusual garden in that the planting style can be described as a generality, since it is extrapolated through all of its spaces. 'I do love planting on a big scale,' Tom admits. The look is not about 'picture-making' in the approved Jekyllian manner, nor of the plantsmen's 'tapestry planting', utilizing a wide range of classic perennials intermixed with rarities. (All of that is rather passé now at this level of English gardening.) Tom's style is light on shrubs and heavy on perennials and grasses planted for structure, something he says he picked up from the likes of Piet Oudolf and Dan Pearson in the mid 1990s. Repetition is key, with sedums, euphorbias, salvias, calamagrostis, miscanthus (mainly *M. sinensis* 'Gracillimus') and clary sage cropping up everywhere, while masses of cranesbill geraniums provide low-level structure. Plantaholic gardeners may turn up their noses at serviceable geraniums, but for Tom they provide a vital structural backbone and rhythm to the whole garden.

Other favourites on this gravelly soil include asphodels and fennel for frothy allure, self-seeded white hesperis, phlox, thalictrums, veronicastrum, eryngiums, eupatoriums, giant alliums, campanulas, helianthus and inulas. Amsonias are a particular favourite at the moment. *Phlomis russeliana*, hollyhocks, foxgloves and shaggy mulleins (*Verbascum olympicum/bombyciferum*) create verticality before the grasses come into their own and really take over in late summer and autumn, offset by the radical fronds and flowers of cardoons and large drifts of purple asters. A few groups of eremerus (foxtail lilies) add drama early in the season, while at the other extreme subtle epimediums can be seen twining through the undergrowth. The colour scheme in spring and early summer is mainly purples and deep blues, with a few splashes of yellow and garnet, notably from *Cirsium rivulare* – still a great favourite among designers – and from aquilegias. Later on, the yellows of inulas, daisy flowers and so on strike a new note. (Tom does not favour pink or orange.)

Nearer the house, Tom has just converted a yew-hedged shrub rose garden into a more detailed continuation of the pervading horticultural theme, with the addition of some elegantly wasted macleayas as a backdrop. 'In smaller spaces you can afford something quite varied,' he explains.

This is a large and diverse plant palette, in the English way, but the overall effect is of simplicity and rigour, because these plants are interwoven with each other in a consistent manner. Jekyll would perhaps have protested that there is no pictorial or narrative structure to this kind of planting, but Tom's intention is to deconstruct the elements of the garden until what is left is a central horticultural theme or tone, extrapolated evenly throughout. 'The garden is stuffed with plants, it's true,' Tom says, 'but I hope people don't come and just gawp at the plants. I hope people will see the spatial progression and above all how the centre is related to the periphery, and then how the whole relates to the landscape surrounding it.' It is a different way of thinking about a garden, but in his own backyard Tom has shown that it can work.

Gardens Illustrated

MIKINORI OGISU
AUGUST 2007
⌇

IN THE AUTUMN OF 1983 Japanese plant-hunter Mikinori Ogisu was, by his own admission, feeling depressed, tired and lonely as he drove his jeep along the treacherous, winding roads of a remote mountain area of south-west Sichuan in China. It was already dusk and there was at least another two hours' driving before he would finally reach the semi-comfort of his hotel – but then he noticed something out of the corner of his eye.

'I saw some late-flowering roses,' he recalls. 'I wasn't feeling very well and I was low in spirits. It was a very difficult time. There had been trouble in getting a special permit from the Chinese government which allowed me to travel in southern Sichuan, and my health was not good – I had lost a lot of weight. But I thought, "It may be something."'

Ogisu slowed the jeep to a halt and parked it precariously on the verge, before climbing laboriously back up the hill to where he had seen the flowers. 'Then I knew,' Ogisu recalls. His instinct had been rewarded with the find of a lifetime: the long-lost China rose, *Rosa chinensis* var. *spontanea*. This semi-mythical plant, with vivid red, star-like flowers, had not been seen in the wild – or anywhere, indeed – for more than half a century, when the plant-hunter Joseph Rock had last described it. Now Ogisu had confirmed yet again his status as the greatest plant-hunter in modern China.

Fellow plant collector Roy Lancaster, in whose kitchen we meet, has known 'Micky' Ogisu for some thirty years and his admiration is clearly unbounded. The consensus is that Ogisu is the most travelled plant explorer in the history of China, making at least six trips a year and regularly contending with rockfalls, crumbling cliff edges and vehicle mishaps. (When I ask him about his worst car crash, he says simply, 'I drove off the cliff.') During twenty-seven years' plant-hunting in China Ogisu estimates that he has covered some two hundred thousand miles, mostly alone, unfunded and unattached to any commercial or academic organization. In fact Ogisu says he has never made a penny out of his plant finds, earning his keep instead as a lecturer, consultant on traditional Japanese garden plants and public park designer.

It is plant collecting which is the focus of his life, however, and he talks of it almost as a spritual quest. Among more than fifty new species which he has discovered, notable finds include a glamorous pink peony, *Paeonia decomposita*, several attractive mahonias (*M. sheridaniana* and *M. leptodonta*), a new evergreen deutzia (*D. multiradiata*), the delicate white-flowered *Bergenia emeiense*, the long-leaved hornbeam *Carpinus fangiana* and any number of epimediums. Ogisu says he prefers to search for plants out of their flowering seasons – which sounds a little perverse until he explains: 'This way I discover the plants which are not easy.' Roy nods sagely in agreement.

Not all of Ogisu's plant successes are the result of derring-do: some are more akin to Poirot-like detection and what Roy describes as Ogisu's respectful approach to the local Chinese people. For example, to find the long-lost Chinese hellebore, *Helleborus thibetanus*, Ogisu followed in the footsteps of nineteenth-century plant-hunter Père David. In the very same village David had mentioned a century earlier, Ogisu showed a dried specimen of the elusive hellebore to local farmers and asked if they had seen it. Met with a blank, Ogisu had a brainwave: 'I told them it was a big white flower which grows straight out of the snow,' he says. 'Then several people said, "Oh, I know it."' They eventually led him to the rocky ground where the plants were growing. 'If you want to find rare plants, look under the stones, because there the temperature is constant, about 16°C,' Ogisu advises. (Roy nods in agreement again and looks wistful – is Ogisu giving away their secrets?)

Ogisu's independent spirit can perhaps be traced back to his upbringing, in a small country town near Nagoya. His father worked as an engineer with Mitsubishi but grew disillusioned during the Second World War when production was turned over to armaments and aeroplanes. After the war he became a carpenter and also practised as what Ogisu calls a 'special monk', living a simple life and ranging across Shintoism, Buddhism and other religions to provide help for people with psychological problems, free of charge. 'My father did something very special,' Ogisu concludes. Perhaps this inspired the son to try to do something equally special; Ogisu explains that his father always taught him to make his own way in the world, to expect nothing from others and to remain utterly focused. 'My father said that school was not important,' he says. 'You can always teach yourself.'

For someone who at first appears to be something of a closed book, Ogisu is in fact unexpectedly direct and honest in explaining how he has single-mindedly pursued his career as a plant collector. He is quite intense when it comes to plants, but good company, too, able to laugh along in the English way.

'So what's next?' I ask, and Ogisu shows me a list of seven cotoneasters which botanists believe are waiting to be rediscovered in China. The challenge is clearly looming large in Ogisu's mind – it's obvious he can't wait to get out there again. This truly is a man with a mission.

Gardens Illustrated

SISSINGHURST AGAIN
JANUARY 2008

·❧·

MOST OF US WOULD AGREE that Sissinghurst remains one of Britain's
– and the world's – favourite gardens, its fame resting on the delights
of its room-like structure and iconic moments such as the White
Garden, but perhaps above all on the personality of Victoria ('Vita')
Sackville-West herself, which still pervades any visit to this romantic
place. Climbing the staircase and entering what was once her room
in the Elizabethan tower that overlooks the garden, it is easy to
imagine Vita as a kind of enchantress, bestowing horticultural glitter
across a garden that spreads out below in flowery hedged enclosures
and mead-like lawns. Sissinghurst is a garden which always seems to
be able to rise to meet the occasion of your own visit, a rare quality
which is perhaps as much the result of the enduring power of Vita's
personality as of continuing horticultural excellence. More venally,
the Vita 'brand' is among the most valuable in gardening, and a few
years ago the National Trust, custodian of Sissinghurst since 1967,
had to introduce a timed-ticket system to cope with visitor demand.

So what was Vita's garden at Sissinghurst all about? Her style did
not simply pop out of nowhere, whatever her fans might suggest.
You could argue that Sissinghurst was essentially the charming
cottage garden 'muddle' promoted equally successfully by Margery
Fish at East Lambrook Manor in Somerset. Vita must also have been
influenced in some way by Gertude Jekyll's technical pronouncements
regarding colour combinations – even if she was only to reject those
prescriptions. Perhaps the cult of the secret garden, which flourished
after publication of Frances Hodgson Burnett's 1911 novel, had
its effect on her thinking, for Sissinghurst is in a way a succession
of secret gardens. We know that Lawrence Johnston's Hidcote had
a profound impact on Vita's planting, particularly in terms of the
'tapestry' effect which remained de rigueur in English gardens until
the mid 1990s. Vita's husband, Harold Nicolson, was a key member

of the so-called 'Foreign Office circle' of men (including Reggie Cooper of Cothay) who were buying up and restoring derelict manor houses in the 1920s and 1930s – and it is important not to overlook the impact of the structure that Nicolson created for the garden. Or perhaps Sissinghurst was conceived more as a writer's fantasy retreat, a horticultural extension of the aristo-bohemianism that was Bloomsbury chic, as displayed at other small country houses such as Charleston and Nether Lypiatt. In this spirit it is possible to trace Vita's exuberant, spontaneous and effusive planting style back through the designs of the kittenish Norah Lindsay (who worked at many of the grandest houses in the 1920s) and to Eleanor Vere Boyle in the late nineteenth century, an unfairly neglected author and gardener who captured the atmosphere of Arts and Crafts planting in a way that her friend Jekyll never did.

The answer, of course, is that Sissinghurst was all of these things, and more besides. Gardens that are based primarily on horticultural materials, and which are created or directed by a single individual, can be viewed as in many ways autobiographies of their owners, in that the hundreds of tiny horticultural decisions which are made every week are inspired by a host of influences from within and without the garden. The gardening style Vita describes in her letters, diaries and columns for the *Observer*, and which can be seen in contemporary photographs of Sissinghurst, is romantic yet practical, experimental but traditional, and in this her approach seemed to chime with that of thousands of other gardeners.

Vita and Harold acquired the derelict Sissinghurst in 1930 and seven years later husband would write to wife: 'We have got what we wanted to get – a perfect proportion between the classic and the romantic, between the element of expectation and the element of surprise.' Nicolson's structural design for the garden, while it does contain room-like elements, is actually quite loose – unpredictable and with plenty of space for surprises. The garden room was not such an innovation, anyway (Vita never pretended it was): gardens are by definition enclosures, and walls and hedges have been garden features in every culture since ancient times. What is important is how this sense of enclosure is used – what effects it was intended to evoke. At Sissinghurst the effect is to add a sense of rhythm, of mystery, of momentum, and – as with all the best performances – of always leaving the audience wanting more. The white garden, the purple border, the spring garden, the nuttery . . . all of these areas flow into each other, linked by the unifying presence of climbing and rambling shrub roses. As Harold wrote to Vita in 1951, reinforcing the gender stereotyping about gardens which seems to find its exemplar at Sissinghurst: 'The bones are there and much of the flesh. Now we must attach rare cosmetics, lovely clothes, and unusual jewellery.'

Perhaps Harold was being a little modest about his manly 'bones', for there is much more statuary and ornament in the garden than is sometimes remembered: most of those narrow brick paths, encroached upon by plants and defined by yew walls, lead to some formal focus, whether it is the shallow, thyme-filled bowl and lion statue of the herb garden, the raised grass dais at the castle end of the rose garden (a clever late addition by Nicolson) or the four columnar yews which anchor the ramshackle priest's house garden.

But what of the garden's atmosphere today – to what extent is Sissinghurst still 'Vita's garden'? The National Trust has been criticized in the past for what some see as an over-manicured approach to the 'ramshackle farm-tumble' (as Harold put it) of Vita's lifetime – and recent reports of 'Keep Off the Flowerbeds' signs do not dispel this reputation. But on the other hand, the garden's status as a hugely popular visitor attraction – with all the health-and-safety worries which that entails – means that it is no longer possible for gardeners to allow, for example, thorny rosebushes to extend themselves across the paths, which have themselves had to be widened and resurfaced to cope with the pedestrian traffic and wheelchairs. Yet a visit to the garden is still extremely rewarding – Vita's life may be fairly recent history, but as with other 'heritage' experiences, you simply have to narrow your eyes and fantasize a little if you want to step back in time and imagine her rounding the corner in her trademark jodphurs and silk blouse, with trug basket and secateurs in hand.

The thorny question of authenticity when it comes to conserving twentieth-century herbaceous gardens is something which the National Trust has yet to address seriously (and I write as a member of the National Trust's gardens advisory panel). Sissinghurst is effectively marketed as 'Vita's garden', when it could be argued that Vita's garden died when she did, in that it was defined by her creative input. The gardeners at Sissinghurst today are being asked to 'method-act', Robert de Niro-style, their way into the mind of this aristocratic bohemian from another age and culture. And for what it is worth, when I raised this problem with Christopher Lloyd at Great Dixter shortly before his death, he agreed that it was effectively impossible to conserve or restore a garden of predominantly herbaceous material in the manner of its creator, after they have gone.

So what is there to do? In practice, what tends to happen is that the garden team tries to work in the spirit of the original creator while also adding something of themselves to the mix. In the end it is almost more a matter of presentation than anything else. But this deference to the past also inhibits innovation, in that gardeners can be reluctant to make changes to a revered garden (when it is really the departed gardener who should be revered, anyway). Perhaps it is time for custodians including the National Trust to face up to the facts of herbaceous perennial gardening, opting to retain certain key features but otherwise push the boundaries as great gardeners have always done in the past. You can't help thinking it is what Vita, for one, would have wanted. As she put it herself in her 1931 poem entitled 'Sissinghurst':

> Beauty, and use, and beauty once again
> Link up my scattered heart, and shape a scheme
> Commensurate with a frustrated dream.

Gardens Illustrated

THREE CHEERS FOR COLOUR
FEBRUARY 2008

SPORADICALLY INTENSE email relationships – we all have them. One of mine is with the Provence-based garden critic and author Louisa Jones, and it is sporadic because it tends to go like this: we get in touch with each other about some reference or favour or query; then one of us mentions an idea in passing; the other person takes issue with it in some way; this develops into a series of essay-length responses on both sides, sometimes getting just a little bit personal. Neither of us minces our words. In fact our words come searing down that email line (or is it a pipe of some sort?) totally unminced. To pursue this unusual butchery metaphor, such messages can become the written equivalent of a hunk of extremely bloody sirloin.

Being a woman, Louisa claims she is being non-aggressive with her critique; while, being a man, I claim I am simply trying to be rational with mine. Neither version is quite right. If ever the 'letters' (emails) between Louisa and me get published – like those of Beth Chatto and Christopher Lloyd – (very unlikely, of course), the volume would not be a gentle ramble entitled 'Dear Friend and Gardener' but something more like 'Dear Complete Pain in the Arse'.

Anyway, during one recent full and frank exchange Louisa and I found something about which we agreed wholeheartedly: colour. Specifically, the way it has been sidelined. 'Yes, three cheers for colour,' her email begins. Living in the south of France, Louisa ostensibly experiences a lot more colour than those of us who are rather farther north – but of course this is one of the easy stereotypes she rails against: 'Although British experts continue to swear that southern light needs bright colours, since only mad dogs and Englishmen go out in the noonday sun, pastels work in fact very well here. As do bright colours. But the latter continue to be linked to flashy vulgarity, and in our case, holiday irresponsibility ("sunny places for shady people" – Somerset Maugham).'

Louisa adds that a French landscape architect of her acquaintance confessed to her that he was ashamed to be found reading one of her luscious, colour-fuelled garden books on the Paris Metro because he felt it was like a form of pornography, while another (male) landscape grandee attacked her for writing seriously about colour. 'His point, made by several other serious landscape architects soon after, was that colour doesn't count. No one but an amateur (and a woman?) would imagine that colour has any role to play in serious design.'

Leaving aside for now the very real issue of gendered attitudes to colour in our culture, it seems to me that bright flora was probably rehabilitated in this country during the decade from about 1996, after years of 'good-taste' gardening in which yellow (in its entirety), for example, was deemed infra dig by the grande dame taste-formers. The catalyst was a combination of the throbbing example of Great Dixter and the rococo moment of English planting design (the Popes' at Hadspen, et al.), which might also be considered the psychedelic phase of the English Home Counties. This extraordinary last gasp of traditional herbaceous planting occurred, of course, just as New Perennials surged (or did it drift?) across the Channel from Holland and Germany. The 'leader' of this movement, Piet Oudolf, quietly and oh-so-heretically affirms time and again that he has no interest in colour and plants purely for form. So where does that leave colour now?

It seems to me that despite the fact that the topic is distinctly unfashionable right now (books on border colour in 1998: 4,321; books on border colour in 2008: nil), most designers and serious amateurs are still pretty much obsessed by it. Many garden on in the Margery Fish 'cottage-muddle' way, regardless of the zeitgeist (a foreign concept, therefore inherently vulgar), while elsewhere the New Perennials look means less tapestry-type design, fewer plant varieties, and drifts or blocks of colours and textures that create a few strident, lasting combinations as opposed to myriad fleeting, serendipitous subtleties. And British gardeners are exploring the possibilities of decay (otherwise known as 'brown'), which is no bad thing. So our obsession with colour has not gone away – it is simply going through a quiet patch.

I can't wait for Louisa's next email.

Garden Design Journal

DUISBURG NORD
NOVEMBER 2008
⟼

PHOTOGRAPHS, texts, first-hand reports, even a lecture by the designers – it quickly transpires that nothing can prepare a visitor for the physical impact, the sheer vastness and complexity, of the landscape park at Duisburg Nord, an ex-ironworks in the industrial Ruhr Valley outside Düsseldorf.

Stepping off the plane and arriving first thing in the morning, for a while I remain rooted to the spot, unable to take in the massiveness of it all: rusting railway wagons sprouting foliage, vast silos and gas-holders, endless warehouses, cranes, chimneys and towers, platforms and pipes, railway lines and canals, elevated walkways and raised tanks, all stretching away farther than the eye could see. On a smaller scale, there are spigots, cranks, pulleys, pumps, wheels, ladders, scoops, cables, fences, handles and scary old notices in German. There is no 'sculpture' here; everything, almost, has been left in place; there are safety barriers, but visitors are more or less left to themselves; the signage relates only to technological matters – there are no aesthetic comments or prompts. One feels like Gulliver in Brobdingnag.

There is still a sense of restless energy about this place, provided partly by the intimations of power and strength exuded by the buildings, and partly by the fecundity of irrepressible plantlife, thriving despite the heavily contaminated soil – birches, buddleia, elder, hawthorn, rowan trees and blackberries sprouting up all over the place. The dynamism of decay. Yet there is a transcendent unity to it all which was identified by the landscape designers – Peter Latz + Partner – at an early stage, for it has been retained and enhanced as its essential atmosphere, the genius of this place. With living things and inanimate materials so sharply juxtaposed, Duisburg Nord is about life, and about death, and also about life after death, for plants now constitute this place as much as buildings ever did. There is no straightforward symbolism here: this is a post-industrial sublime.

First, some facts. The Duisburg plant was constructed between 1898 and 1910 by industrial magnate August Thyssen and became the largest ironworks in Europe, manufacturing 1,000 tons of pig iron per day. It was closed down in 1985 but saved from demolition after massive local protest. Latz + Partner won the competition to re-landscape the site and put their plans into action through the 1990s, with the park opening to the public in 1994. It covers five acres and comprises a dizzying array of post-industrial buildings and other features, many of which have been subject to subtle landscape interventions by Latz or else put to entirely new leisure uses: the gasometer is now a diving tank; the old ore bunkers have been made into climbing walls and children's slides; you can learn to walk the high wire in the blast furnaces.

Cowperplatz draws the visitor in: a grid of cherry trees which creates an understorey level that mediates the vastness and hardness of the structures, their height now partly obscured by leaves. Beyond here lies the heart of the park, and the most decisive intervention by the designers: Piazza Metallica. This is a large open space named by Latz in honour of the massive rusted brown iron plates which form a simple chessboard-like grid in the centre. These were once used to cover pig-iron casting moulds, and are scarred and pockmarked like geological phenomena. The result is akin to a piece of land art. The piazza can contain some fifty thousand people and is often used for events and gatherings. From here one can gain a fine view of the complex panorama of pipes and different shapes which constantly unfolds around the visitor, like some vast accidental walk-through sculptural installation. Adjacent is the steam blast house, now a spectacular bar and events venue; Duisburg Nord is a public space which is enthusiastically used.

Most visitors head straight for Blast Furnace No.5. This towering structure is no antique – it was built in 1973 – and it gives the visitor the unmatchable opportunity to climb seventy metres up its platforms and survey the whole park. Inside, a cavernous chamber contains the remains of the smelting works, with massive chains hanging above deep vats and furnaces, for this is the heaviest of heavy industry. Old control panels look like something from 1960s sci-fi.

Beyond lies the Ore Bunker Gallery, a huge cellular structure visible via elevated metal walkways, and beyond that the Clear Water Canal, as it was renamed by Latz, which is crisscrossed by bridges. Some locals wanted this canal turned into a naturalistic stream as a 'healing' gesture, but Latz argued that that would drain it of all meaning – so it was simply cleaned and then re-opened. The Sinterplatz north of the canal is the site of a tall wind turbine and a series of entirely enclosed, almost monastic (in feel) gardens which are Latz's prime horticultural interventions – formal spaces of hedges, perennials and herb plantings which can only be viewed from the long metal walkway that runs above. From this part of the park one gets the best view of a huge, rusted-brown double pipe on tall supports which slashes a horizontal line across the entire landscape – a sculptural intervention on a scale of which most artists could only dream.

Spreading westwards in the direction of the canal is a series of near parallel paths – the poetically named Harp Strings – which follow old railway lines. These provide a more bucolic savour – with weeds and wildflowers (fireweed, ragwort, brambles, nettles) on the quiet verges – as well as a chance to enjoy long views back towards the plant itself. It gives the visitor a chance to get some perspective, literally and metaphorically.

All kinds of meanings can be read into Latz's many and various interventions. Are the trees planted round the base of the gasometer really a reference to Rousseau's tomb on the island of Ermenonville? Perhaps such a knowing interpretation is not particularly relevant when one can enjoy the sensual contrast of giant rivets with soft, peeling bark, or compare the slender trunks to the vertical metal posts stretching fifty metres into the air.

So what was the designers' philosophy? Landscape architects – and particularly perhaps German male landscape architects – like to create pseudo-scientific 'systems' which explain (and legitimize) their work. Latz + Partner have duly developed what they call a 'syntax' of landscape (the title of a new book on their work by Udo Weilacher), which refers to a coherent, unifying language or tonal attitude which can be seen in both the natural and manmade elements of the post-industrial spaces in which they now specialize.

Put simply, Latz is reacting against the romantic idea that the plants and trees which have been colonizing such places are somehow in harmony with industry despite their apparent antipathy to it, or (even worse) are somehow cleansing or redeeming this 'contaminated' industrial space. Latz's argument is that nature and industry (or 'technology' as he puts it) can be seen to be working in exactly the same spirit and direction, with a minimum of design intervention, towards a common end which is the landscape park itself.

This is a difficult message to sell in these times of eco-guilt, when self-recrimination at mankind's apparent destruction of the planet is in vogue. But Latz's statement is powerful, and the basic sense that emerges – that nature and landscape are acting as equal partners here in every way – can be understood instinctively by every single visitor.

Gardens Illustrated

AMERICAN ALLIGATORS
JANUARY 2009
<small>↢</small>

A RECENT ARTICLE about Thomas Jefferson's garden reminded me of my own visits to gardens in the United States, including Monticello. There is something quite distinctive about the American garden-making tradition, and I have been trying to puzzle out what that is while putting together a book on the subject. It has something to do with the American attitude towards wilderness, formed as it was during the earliest days of colonization and subsequently honed by writers including Thoreau and Emerson, and more recently by the likes of Michael Pollan (in *Second Nature*).

For sure there is a strong moral and religious element to it, as Jefferson himself opined: 'Those who labor in the earth are the chosen people of God . . . Corruption of morals in the mass of cultivators is a phenomenon of which no age or nation has furnished an example.'

I am not sure how many 'cultivators' you know who are utterly devoid of sin, but I think I understand what the president was getting at. The way of gardening over the pond perhaps reflects a typically American cast of mind: that can-do optimism about the future in general and in this context man (and woman)'s ability to bend pristine wilderness to their own agricultural and economic ends. The frontier mentality of making do with what is available and living within nature rather than in opposition to it is strongly reflected in American garden making, which has always contained an element of sturdy practicality (witness the experimental fruit and veg gardens at Monticello). This can be seen on a smaller scale in the tradition of 'yard gardening' in small-town America, where decoration has traditionally taken second place to practical considerations – in earlier days food production but latterly encompassing barbecues, hot tubs and basketball hoops.

The American mode of gardening is framed, then, by the nation's historic embrace of the wilderness ideal. The way that garden-makers in America have traditionally sought to embrace the natural world, to invite it into their garden spaces, is quite at odds with the European tradition, which has generally been focused on an attempt to fence it out by means of sequestered enclosures. Even the English landscape park, an ostensibly 'naturalistic' approach to garden making, had as its object a highly particular version of the pastoral which often involved the redevelopment of the existing topography.

In America, even in cases where the detail of the design was initially inspired by European examples, it seems to me that the beckoning natural landscape will often be harnessed to set the tone of the garden as a whole.

* * *

IF THESE MUSINGS seem a little rarified, perhaps there is consolation in the fact they have been hard-won at times. Take my visit to the extraordinary eighteenth-century water garden at Middleton Place in South Carolina. I had travelled south from Virginia on the overnight Amtrak train in the mistaken belief that this mode of travel would somehow be more civilized and romantic than flying. Wrong: my tiny 'first-class' sleeper cabin looked like a death-row cell designed for some murderous midget. And just as I was trying to get to sleep the first massive jolt occurred, lifting me bodily off the thin mattress into the night air. This continued all night. (I was later told the long-distance trains use freight routes in the South, hence the rough ride.) The Orient Express it was not, though at times I wished someone (or, indeed, everyone) would just come along and kill me.

I arrived at Charleston in a predictably addled state at 5.30 a.m. A taxi took me to my destination: the extraordinary eighteenth-century water garden of Middleton Place. The reception desk at the hotel connected to the property was deserted so I decided to take a preliminary early-morning stroll round the garden, which is set on the banks of the Ashley River amid the swampy remains of ricefields from plantation days. It was a glorious morning, with shafts of impossibly bright sunshine lighting up dew droplets in the grass. Then I saw the sign:

ALLIGATORS

It did not say 'Beware the Alligators', as surely it should have done, but took a more informational tack, explaining that these giant reptiles roam around the place in groups of up to two hundred and are in fact altogether charming, contrary to every basic human instinct. I immediately legged it (or 'high-tailed it', in local parlance) up a ladder and on to one of the wooden viewing platforms erected for viewing these creatures. Can alligators climb ladders? I wondered. Or are they, like daleks, flummoxed by steps?

The coast appeared clear and I made it back to reception where I was told that the alligators were completely harmless. 'Yeah, right,' I thought (well, this was America).

Later that day, after I had spent several hours exploring the garden, I overheard a conversation between the man whose job it was to look after the sheep and other livestock at the estate's model farm and a visitor who was asking him whether the sheep ever got to graze on the lush pasture near the river. 'We never let them down there,' he replied. 'The alligators take them.' So it transpired that these animals were not harmless vegetarians, after all . . .

I was going to relate how I was later attacked by a swarm of killer bees in the Italianate gardens of Vizcaya in Miami, but re-living the alligator experience has proved more than enough for now.

***

ANOTHER 'ISSUE' around garden visiting in America is the almost complete absence of public transport. Arranging a visit to Longwood gardens, near Philadelphia, I was perplexed to be told by both the garden and my hotel (almost next door, albeit along the freeway) that it was 'impossible' to get to the garden without a car. The only option – other than hiring a car, which I was determined not to do – was to summon a taxi from the nearest city, entailing a thirty-mile round trip for the one-mile journey. I decided against this and resolved to walk there – somehow.

Leaving soon after dawn, I embarked on a commando-style mission. Objective: to find a way to the garden along the edge of the freeway. It meant skirting round parking lots, striding across the springy front lawns of nail-care parlors, trekking past gas stations and hacking through areas of thick woodland which looked like crime scenes waiting to happen. At one point, as I scrambled along fairly close to the hard shoulder, a police patrol car seemed to take an interest in me. I melted into the foliage, Rambo-like (if I may say so). I eventually reached Longwood via a cemetery.

Longwood is the greatest horticultural extravaganza in America, created by Pierre du Pont of the Pennsylvania chemicals dynasty in the early twentieth century. The great conservatory alone takes up five acres and there are no fewer than three monumental fountain displays which are set off for visitors' delectation every day. Even the local Amish community comes to visit.

After all this fun I returned to my hotel the same way, dodging through the undergrowth. I felt vindicated but had a nagging suspicion that my perfectly rational approach to environmentally friendly garden visiting may have appeared a little 'unusual' to some.

Country Life

VILLA GAMBERAIA
MARCH 2009
↭

THE CELEBRATED GARDEN of Villa Gamberaia overlooks Florence some five miles from the city centre, just beyond the village of Settignano. It emerges as one of the most finely balanced of all garden designs – a property of small size, just three acres, which is nevertheless possessed of breathtaking variety.

Records are scant but we know that the four-square, typically Tuscan villa was constructed in 1610 by the Lapi family, when the house would have been surrounded by orchards and fields. The word *gamberaia* translates as crayfish pool, once a common enough feature in the hills above Florence. A century later the property passed to the Capponi family, who developed it further – we know from an estate map that the essential layout and all the key decorative features were in place by 1725. The garden as it stands today is a remarkable survival: it was rescued from dereliction in the 1950s by Marcello Marchi and is now cared for in the same exemplary spirit by his son-in-law, Dr Luigi Zalum. Gamberaia now exudes that comfortably mellow atmosphere which seems to arise only in gardens which have been cared for by the same family over generations.

Iron gates open to reveal a cypress avenue leading up to the house, the terrace of its west front providing wonderful, hazy views across the valley of the Arno (this is a garden which boasts views on three sides). Olive groves come right up to the base of the terrace, as they have always done.

The main water parterre to the south, an early twentieth-century addition which has grown to appear almost timeless, contains four rectangular pools surrounded by clipped box hedges and yew columns which in their form seem to ripple away in rhythm with the garden's basic plan. There are lavender, santolina, roses and lilies here, but the parterre's general appearance is overwhelmingly green. The space ends in a U-shaped pool enveloped by a low 'amphitheatre' of box hedges and a loggia-like 'belvedere' of clipped cypresses, but perhaps the cleverest aspect of the design is the width of its central aisle, which makes the parterre as pleasant to walk in as it is to look at from above.

Villa Gamberaia became well known in the opening decades of the twentieth century, in large part due to the attraction of the water parterre and its creators: the eccentric, reclusive Princess Ghyka (a Romanian aristocrat whose sister was the queen of Serbia) and her American companion, Flora Blood. A visit to Villa Gamberaia became a must for any rich and well-connected American visitor and several of them were directly inspired by its example. Together with Bernard Berenson's Villa I Tatti (almost next door), Arthur Acton's La Pietra and Lady Sybil Cutting's Villa Medici at Fiesole, Gamberaia became a social focus for an intense band of arty ex-pats who had been drawn to Florence.

The most unusual and innovative element of Gamberaia's garden design is the so-called 'bowling green'. Flanked by high walls, this uncompromising axis bisects the property along its entire length – 225 metres. At its northern end, circled by cypresses, is a nymphaeum with a curious rockwork motif of a devillish figure holding a trident, flanked by lions. Derived from designs by the sixteenth-century designer Niccolò Tribolo, the symbolism here is a mixture of references to Neptune, the sea god, and Pan, god of the forests.

After the openness of the bowling green, the intimacy of the tufa-encrusted rockwork cabinet adjacent comes as the pleasantest of shocks. This is a strikingly narrow space on multiple levels, where obelisks, statues and numerous classical busts emphasize verticality, adding greatly to the visual excitement. With an inviting sandstone balustrade above, it is possible to view this tiny space from seemingly any angle. At Gamberaia, a choice is always followed by a surprise, and there are at least seven routes out of the cabinet, each with a different tonal conclusion. One, for example, takes the visitor right around the apsidal space at the far end, behind a great two-handled basin, where once upon a time water jets would suddenly soak the visitor. Another choice brings the visitor up a staircase and into the south *selvatico* (decorative woodland) via a dark, right-angled portal, with a surprise view out across the olive groves. The two *selvatici* at Gamberaia are thick with holm oaks and bear many traces of seats, tiny glades and other diversions; they remain extremely atmospheric.

Occupying a platform-like space above the rockwork cabinet is the lemon garden and the huge *limonaia* itself: in summer this area presents an orderly array of magnificent citrus plants in their massive terracotta pots, with some attractive herbaceous perennial plantings in the beds surrounding, including climbing rose 'Albertine', oleanders, achillea varieties, agapanthus, daylilies and numerous tree peonies.

The genius of Villa Gamberaia's garden lies in its balance, and the key to that balance is provided by the presence of the bowling green, which acts not only as a fulcrum but as a palette cleanser, allowing a variety of spaces with quite different atmospheres to thrive alongside each other. As a result the garden seems to communicate with the visitor on a personal level. It seems one's relationship with Villa Gamberaia can be nothing but intimate, for this is a garden which speaks in nothing but whispers.

Gardens Illustrated

DOWN WITH DESIGN

MARCH 2009

DOWN WITH DESIGN. That may seem a strange sentiment to read in a professional design journal but the thought occurred to me forcibly while I was listening to Dan Pearson speak recently. It was one of the most articulate and thoughtful talks I have heard in a long time. Here, however, I want to refer less to what he was actually saying than to how he was saying it.

While Dan was describing his recent projects in Japan and elsewhere, there was never any possibility that he was going to mention the 'D' word as some kind of component in the work – 'design' as the drawing-board stage, say, of any given project, to be considered alongside other quotidian aspects of a company's life such as client liaison and professional development. It was clear that every 'design' decision Dan was making came from somewhere deep within him, so that it emerged instinctively and quite often spontaneously as an entirely authentic expression of his personality. Everything else followed on from that. It made the whole notion of self-conscious 'design' seem somehow redundant or perhaps rather incidental, an element of craft (and graft) which all professional designers ought to master as a given before allowing their own personal vision to take over. It occurred to me that 'design' ought to be something learned in college, almost as a set of practical techniques to be honed and practised until they become second nature and then held in the mind effortlessly, allowing deeper ideas to percolate through the whole person and into the work as it appears on the ground. At that point, one's 'design style' becomes less a range of skills, personal mannerisms and preferences, more akin to a mode of being, a way of relating to the world as a whole – a manner of thinking, of speaking, of making marks on paper and of manipulating materials on site. Perhaps it is only when a designer reaches this point that the transition from competent professional to visionary maker might be made.

This apparent absence of 'design' in a maker's aesthetic vocabulary is something which can be detected, in different ways, in the personalities of many top garden designers and landscape architects. Steve Martino in Arizona, whom I happened to interview recently, has this quality in spades. He says he is entirely nonplussed when people refer to his way of working as a 'design philosophy' – in his case the use of the local desert flora in conjunction with expressive Modernist hardscaping – because it sounds as if it is a formula he applies, as opposed to his instinctive way of being and working, honed over some thirty-five years' experience. Yes, in some cases such an attitude can mean that a designer gives an impression of arrogance, as if they are living in their own bubble, swallowing only their own self-generated hype, and I know this can be frustrating to garden writers. But it is not really the job of critics to teach designers how to think more 'critically', in terms of the way they might fit into the pattern of garden and landscape design worldwide. Though some of them obviously can, designers ought not to be expected to talk or write intelligibly about their own work, let alone anyone else's. It is the work that matters.

Modernists may rail at this idea of the redundancy of 'good design' as an end destination because it is an essentially anti-functionalist point of view that mitigates against the idea that design is a rational process which can be taught and learned on principle as an end in itself. That is the mode of thinking which still prevails in our design schools, partly because it is quite straightforward to teach. It means that designers who have come through that educational process may be loath to let go of the tenets of 'good design' which have helped get them where they are in their careers. But I would argue that an emphasis on design above all – with the chimerical 'good design' as a professional Holy Grail – will only get us so far. We talk about 'good design' all the time, as if that is the end of the process, when in reality it is merely a set of tools which might be used in the creation of something that is really important. So much garden design, even work which is perfectly competent on the face if it, seems anaemic and derivative, because a designer has not found a way of expressing a personality, a way of speaking to us directly through the work. Down with design.

Garden Design Journal

IAN HAMILTON FINLAY
APRIL 2009
⌁

WHO WILL READ *Nature Over Again* by John Dixon Hunt? It falls between two stools, gardening and art, just like its subject, the late Ian Hamilton Finlay. He was the creator, over forty-five years, of Little Sparta, near Edinburgh, generally acknowledged to be the most important garden created in the late twentieth century in Britain, if not the world. Hunt describes it as 'the ultimate realization' of the work of the artist. But it is still not very widely known outside the world of gardens. Why?

The problem facing gardening, in terms of its position in the hierarchy of the arts, is that while a cheery character like Alan Titchmarsh may not seem to have much in common with a serious artist-gardener like Ian Hamilton Finlay, when it comes to the topic of gardening it is the Titchmarsh end of the equation which looms largest in the public's mind – as it does, too, in the minds of almost all arbiters of cultural taste. (The Arts Council, for example, will not give grants to garden projects – though as Finlay himself put it in 1980 after one of his spats with that body: 'What is the Arts Council but a sordid rabble of lords, lawyers, ex-lawyers, and office boys?')

Imagine how outraged the art world would be if Rolf Harris – as opposed to, say, Lucian Freud – was perceived, among the cultural elite, to be a high point of contemporary art? Anyone who thinks seriously about gardens must put up with that kind of thing. Perhaps it is because, as an artistic environment, the garden militates against certain dearly held art world pieties which also happen to be commercially expedient, including the primacy of the artist as a creative force (in gardens the weather tends to get in the way of that) and the artist as the creator of an immutable art object (the materials used in gardens change all the time, as does the environment).

These very factors serve to make Finlay's *œuvre* seem all the more important and urgent at this time, when the prospect of ecological armageddon, and perhaps more importantly our collective guilt over that, has emerged as a defining idea of the age. One would imagine that in such a context a garden might be viewed as a potentially useful artistic environment, since the garden is historically the most piquant and intimate cultural arena in which humans have interacted with nature.

Hunt, as an academic garden historian, is alive to the reluctance of critics in 'related' disciplines to engage with gardens, and draws attention to the perceived impertinence (his word) of those who would seek to elevate the status of garden making above that of hobby. Yet, like Finlay himself, he soon leaves these irritations behind and embarks on a discursive meander through the key works: Little Sparta, Stockwood Park in Luton and the late work Fleur de l'Air in Provence, a private garden which has until now seemed rather mysterious (its revelation is one of the chief recommendations of the book). Hunt uses as a guide Finlay's notion of the garden as an 'attack', an idea drawn from one of his more celebrated epigrams: 'Certain gardens are described as retreats when they are really attacks.' In other words, while many gardens can be appreciated in an intellectually passive state because they are chiefly hedonistic (as in the English tradition of flower gardening), in others the visitor has the option of engagement with a programme of symbolism or meaning (as in the early eighteenth-century English landscape garden, or Finlay's own work).

In sixteen short, clearly focused chapters, the author describes the various ways Finlay uses material artefacts – chiefly fragments, inscriptions and sculptures – in the garden to point up the complexities and contradictions of human nature and society in general, as well as the poetic method which gives rise to his allusive inscriptions and witty wordplays. By means of the insertion of words and objects in gardens (notably at Little Sparta), Finlay creates a continuous oscillation between pastoral benevolence and militaristic malevolence – hand-grenade gatepost finials, or a submarine emerging from a clump of hostas, juxtaposed with classically inspired poetic fragments. One moving example of the latter which may well be new to readers is the six Eurydice stones at Fleur de l'Air in Provence, inscribed:

EURYDICE THE WOODS

EURYDICE THE FLOODS
EURYDICE THE SNOWS

EURYDICE THE MOUNTAIN-TOPS
EURYDICE THE STARS

EURYDICE THE GROVES
EURYDICE THE SWIFTS

EURYDICE THE NIGHTINGALES
EURYDICE THE CLOUDS

EURYDICE THE OAKS
EURYDICE THE ROCKS

Meanings do not always leap out of Finlay's inscriptions or printed works. A phrase such as, 'Camouflage is the last form of classical landscape painting' sounds lightly epigrammatic but might also be considered overly gnomic (as such it is the closest we will get to a gnome in a Finlay garden), but is always decipherable, a process made easier if one has entered into Finlay's 'zone' of inference. On one level, Hunt's book works as a helpmeet into that zone. There is a delightfully spontaneous feel to the writing which leads to fresh insights about Finlay's work as well as numerous observations which are useful in the aesthetic appreciation of gardens in general.

Hunt lights upon Ovid, the poet of transformation, as the presiding poetic deity in Finlay's gardens, and to this end demonstrates what he calls 'the possibility of multiple interpretations' in the work: the existence of numerous yet specific potential interpretations. Which is not the same thing at all as ambiguity. Hunt describes himself as flummoxed on one or two occasions by Finlay's inscriptions (he spends a whole chapter wondering what Finlay may have meant by 'Mower is Less', a pun on Mies van der Rohe's dictum) but he never implies that Finlay himself may not have felt the necessity to know the answer. Ultimately Finlay is revealed as profoundly non-ironic in attitude, which is saying something for an artist who was in his pomp in the 1980s. In conclusion Hunt compares Finlay's delicate technique favourably with that seen in most contemporary public art: 'Some of Finlay's most engaging work as a garden-maker consists of these minimal hints by which we gain more, larger understanding; it perhaps also explains his objection to the heavy-handed insertions of sculpture in attempts to beef up the otherwise unmediated world of nature.' (The latest such 'insertion' to be announced is surely Mark Wallinger's monumental, and monumentally trite, white horse sculpture in Kent, which is intended to impress Eurostar passengers as they approach London.)

The one area which Hunt unduly neglects in this book is that of politics. The fact that Finlay was a political artist, and that his political stance was provocatively discomforting, has been consistently downplayed by his critics. But here is an artist who freely employed Nazi imagery and recruited some of the 'heroes' of the French Revolution to his cause, as the official artist to his own republic of the mind, and of his own threatened demesne at Little Sparta. Hunt expends just a few sentences on the figure of Antoine Saint-Just, author of the phrase inscribed on massive stones which act as the climax of Little Sparta – 'The Present Order is the Disorder of the Future' – who also doubles up as the great golden head of Apollo inscribed 'Apollon Terroriste'. But Saint-Just was probably the most enthusiastic guillotiner of the new republic, responsible for hundreds if not thousands of deaths in a few hysterical weeks (he lost his own head shortly afterwards).

One could argue that Finlay used the figure of Saint-Just to personify the tension between idealism and cruelty, and that is true on one level – but this is the starring role of the garden. And 'The Present Order . . .' quotation could be read as both apocalyptic and vengeful. Is there really nothing more to say? Finlay-affiliated critics close ranks, however, while an uncharacteristically weak-minded Hunt opines: 'It is sometimes difficult to grasp exactly what Finlay wants us to understand from his references to the historical events of the Revolution'.

This reluctance to engage with politics among Finlay's critics emerged again last year when I chaired a discussion at the Garden Museum in London. The three panellists had known Finlay well and are now trustees of Little Sparta. They are protective of his legacy in a physical sense, in the shape of the garden, on an intellectual level of course, but also in terms of his personal character. Finlay was an artist who inspired and encouraged discipleship; in the early 1980s he invited various friends – most of them fellow artists and writers – to join his so-called Committtee of Public Safety at Little Sparta. This functioned as a moral, artistic and at times physical riposte to the cultural vandalism being committed by his local council which, almost unbelievably, was resorting to forcible repossession of sculptural works at Little Sparta because of Finlay's refusal to pay business rates on his premises. (The artist argued that his Temple of Apollo, a former outhouse which acted as a kind of gallery, was a religious building and therefore exempt from the tax.) Those who were involved speak fondly of this heroic period in Finlay's career; it cemented loyalty among his followers.

Perhaps as a result of this loyalty, every time I tried to raise with 'Team Finlay' the difficult subject of politics in the work, the question was blanked or sidestepped. I am told it was rather like listening to the maneouvrings of politicians on the radio. Of course Finlay's cheerleaders have good reason to be wary because it was the 'discovery' of Finlay's use of Nazi imagery (specifically the SS symbol) which led to his being dropped from a key artistic role in France's 1989 Revolution celebrations. The subsequent denigration of Finlay as some kind of neo-fascist, coupled with the feeling that the French episode may have stalled his international career, has led to a culture of silence on this aspect of his work. A silence which could in fact be construed by those same denigrators as an admission of Finlay's culpability.

Finlay himself was more alive to the artistic potential of this topic than any of his critics have been; it led to his long correspondence and near-collaboration with the imprisoned Albert Speer, Hitler's architect. Here was an official artist beholden to a vaunting ideology, which is precisely what Finlay considered himself to be. Finlay imposed upon himself a role as a public or official artist of sorts – in this case as the representative of a 'state' which might also be described as the state of mind of the artist. In the end *Nature Over Again* covers Finlay's methodology well, but once again the politics has been missed, when politics was close to the heart of Finlay's work.

Perhaps the next generation of critics, those who have not enjoyed tea and conversation with the artist at Little Sparta, or manned the barricades with him against Strathclyde District Council, will be better placed to address such themes in Finlay's work. In the meantime, if people don't want to talk about the politics, there is always the weather. After all, as Finlay once suggested, 'Weather is the chief content of a garden.'

Literary Review

MUSIC AND GARDENS
APRIL 2009
↢

IN A CONCERT HALL, listening to Mahler's Symphony No. 9, the first movement of which seems to embody a whole world in itself, I found myself reflecting on what it is that gardens have to offer that music does not, and vice versa. It is striking how many garden designers, past and present, have found musical analogies to be a useful way of describing their own work and design method. For them, the garden's cadences and motifs intermingle and interact with each other in a way that is strongly reminiscent of music.

Of course there is a certain fluidity inherent in music which makes such comparisons attractive. Gardens change, music changes, so that the impression with both can be of unfettered spontaneity and wholly natural, organic growth. In the case of orchestral music and flower gardens, one has an impression of many and various elements conspiring together to create a complex yet coherent whole, which might well seem to be possessed of its own self-sustaining creative mechanism. There is a sense that gardeners and composers alike are trying to marshal vital forces over which they have only minimal control – though in both cases that impression will often be illusory.

Or is it the case that garden designers are in reality closer to conductors, in that they do not exactly write the scripts for the plants they use but can only prepare in advance and then try to guide them in real time?

One of the reasons why musical analogies are popular is that gardens so often seem to contain multiple themes, some of which become more apparent in certain seasons – just as specific aspects of a piece of music might suddenly hove into (aural) view after a gap between listens, or simply as we get older. It's that idea of mutability and changefulness again. A phrase which becomes a theme or motif in a piece of music can be compared with the repetition of a plant or a combination of plants in a border design; or, on a larger scale, the pervading tone of a piece written for a solo instrument might find its equivalent in a particularly intense and personal garden environment. Even a highly unusual garden, such as Dan Kiley's Modernist masterpiece at the Miller House in Columbus, Indiana – which I happen to have visited recently – might find its musical sibling. Kiley's design is extraordinary because in it he sought for a flat hierarchy of spaces, a garden without focal points or highlights but an evenness of tone which engenders an intensely Arcadian atmosphere. The musical equivalent here clearly cannot be Beethoven and could not even be Bach – perhaps it is the programmatic music of Philip Glass or Steve Reich? Yes, this is a parlour game, but it may be of more use than that. Coherence is all, and the best music, the best abstract art – and the best gardens – always cohere.

Actually what I was really thinking about as I listened to the Mahler was what gardens do *not* offer us, in comparison with music. That piece seems to have the ability to communicate directly with the listener certain very specific emotions and emotional states, in a way that gardens simply cannot. Music can create the impression of intense and particular human interaction – with the composer and his/her thoughts, which in reality means oneself – while with gardens there is always a distance, a sense that the creator is there, but present as a kind of presiding spirit rather than as a living companion into whose mind you have crept. But this sense of distance – of alienation from conventional ideas about human creative processes – does have its advantages. Not the least is that it gives the garden visitor the impression that alongside all the plants and materials they can see, and all the human interactions with the place of which they may be aware, visitors themselves are important elements in the life of the garden, since by the very fact of their presence they become co-creators of the sense of place. That participatory element is what sets gardens apart from other art forms. It requires makers to cede a good deal of artistic control in the process – though not, one hopes, the artistic credit.

Garden Design Journal

GREAT DIXTER
MAY 2009
⧼⧽

WHEN CHRISTOPHER LLOYD DIED on 27 January 2006, the gardening world lost its most respected and iconoclastic plantsman and author. Many at that point wondered what would become of his celebrated garden, Great Dixter in Sussex. Would it be turned into a hotel, like Rosemary Verey's Barnsley House, or be taken on by the National Trust and lose much of its personality, as at Vita Sackville-West's Sissinghurst? Would this once-famous garden be well tended yet lapse into local-authority obscurity, as has E.A.Bowles's Myddelton House, or would it simply be left to wither away, like a number of other once-great twentieth-century gardens?

Until almost the end of his life this last, hard option seemed the obvious route to Christo (as he was always known). He had a horror of those gardens where an attempt is made to maintain the place 'in the spirit' of an owner who is long dead. But this most opinionated of gardeners was not above a change of heart and, as he explained to me at Dixter just a few months before he died, he was by then thinking seriously about how the garden might best be continued after he had gone.

The house at Dixter was built – well, cobbled together – out of several architectural fragments in 1910 by Christo's father,

Nathaniel, in collaboration with the great architect Edwin Lutyens. The garden structure of curving yew hedges on sloping ground was barely altered by Christo, leaving him free to experiment with the plants which were his real passion.

People were another abiding interest, and although Christo tended to be as discriminating – or as high-handed, depending on one's point of view – about them as he was about plants, this lifelong bachelor drew about himself a wide and varied circle of friends who would regularly gather at his home. These friends are perhaps the key to the garden's future, since a group of them have formed a board of trustees led by John Watkins (also head of gardens at English Heritage) which is now working to ensure its survival not only as an experimental flower garden but as an important building in the Arts and Crafts tradition, and as a place where promising young gardeners can learn their craft.

The most important factor of all in the Great Dixter equation does not appear on a spreadsheet, however, but comes in the form of Fergus Garrett, Christo's head gardener for the last fifteen years of his life and the man now in overall charge of house and garden. He lives not at Dixter but in Hastings with his wife and two children. And, as he explains to me while we wander through the High Garden, it was vital for Fergus that he had Christo's blessing to continue the experimental spirit of the garden.

'For years Christo said he didn't care what happened to the garden after his death,' Fergus recalls. 'Then one day he said to me, "You are the future of Great Dixter." Later, when he was dying, he said, "I do hope you will stay on." He said the fifteen years he had had with me had been the happiest of his life. I said to him that if Dixter changes in ways I didn't like, I would leave. He said, "That's fine." '

'Actually,' Fergus continues, 'the easy thing would have been to leave. But I thought: I haven't finished here. There's so much to do. And if Dixter ever bored me, or changed for the worse, I'd leave tomorrow.'

The key to the garden's originality and verve is partly due to the working method laid down by Christo. This consisted of a daily perambulation round the garden which lasted about an hour, during which time Christo and Fergus would make perhaps sixty decisions, small and large. About half of them were to be dealt with immediately, the rest stored up for the right seasonal moment.

'Everything was looked at and carefully considered,' Fergus says. 'We asked: is it worth it? Does it grow well? Does it stand on its own?' That discriminating method is how such exciting Dixter combinations as red tulips against lime-green euphorbia came to be, or the symphony of dots that is forget-me-nots within cotoneaster. Fergus says he continues this tradition today, only now it involves the entire garden staff and lasts all day. 'This is not a fluffy cottage garden that just continues smoothly on,' he points out. 'It's a place where we've always been expressive. I love this fast-track gardening. I love the quirkiness of big plants and big veg (although Christo thought that was gross), the sense of the countryside being let in.'

As we stop and peruse various plantings around the garden, it becomes clear that for Fergus it is perfectly natural to continue in this tradition – anything else would seem strange. But he is also allowing his own horticultural voice to sing out, especially in the emphasis on what he calls 'link plants', including thalictrum, forget-me-nots, bronze fennel and that Dixter signature plant, *Verbena bonariensis*. 'Christo would never have allowed this,' Fergus says, gesturing across a border interspersed with cow parsley, and later, a corner beset by spreading *Anemone ranunculoides*. 'I'm more self-sown oriented than he was.' Later, we come across an unusual epimedium, carefully tended – 'He hated those!' Fergus exclaims.

The sense of authenticity that prevails at Great Dixter is partly due to Fergus's insistence on no signage, no gift shop, modest plant sales, a no-frills car park (with a superb view) and a general emphasis on keeping things as they have been. But it can mainly be attributed to a confidence in his own decision-making.

'I do stop and wonder what Christo would think,' Fergus reflects. 'But if I decide he wouldn't approve, it doesn't stop me. I do it anyway. Because that is how we worked after the first five years. He'd say,

"Okay, you prove to me it works." In the last few years he let me try whatever I wanted. He'd sometimes say, "Oh, you'll grow out of it."'

Great Dixter's head gardener is now a chief executive and a celebrity in his own right, in great demand for lectures around the world. But one senses he is still deeply immersed in a daily dialogue with a close colleague who also happened to be his employer. 'Christo is not hovering over my shoulder,' Fergus quietly remarks. 'He is by my side.'

Daily Telegraph

THE SHEFFIELD SCHOOL
JUNE 2009

RECENTLY a rather jaded garden writer came up to me and said, 'So what's the next big thing? New Perennials is all over.' I'm not sure about New Perennials being over (it's just being absorbed in different ways into our planting tradition), but arguably the next big thing in this country is shaping up to be what I would term the 'Sheffield School' of planting.

This is a group of academics and researchers based at Sheffield University, led by James Hitchmough and Nigel Dunnett, who are pioneering an even more naturalistic planting style than any of the incarnations of New Perennials we have seen so far. Where the Sheffield School departs from the look promulgated by Piet Oudolf, the late Henk Gerritsen et al. is in the way they seek to allow plantings to create their own internal dynamism – to design themselves, essentially. They are not thinking in terms of drifts of plants working together through the seasons, or of bold combinations of tried and tested ornamental grasses and perennials, but seeding areas in accordance with scientifically worked out matrices derived from looking at specific plant communities in the wild, from Chile to South Africa to Australia to the Steppes. They light the blue touchpaper, as it were, and then stand back, only intervening in later seasons if it appears things are going badly wrong (when a single species appears to be taking over, for example).

This new form of 'design-less design' might justifiably set alarm bells ringing among professional garden designers: it does sound a little like a negation of human artistic intervention in gardens and landscape, ceding all control to nature in this way. New Perennials remains heretical enough for many garden designers in Britain, in that a central tenet espoused by Oudolf is that plants are not selected for their colour qualities, either as specimens or in combination with others, but solely for their form. That effectively throws out of the window a century and more of British herbaceous border development, which as we know has mainly been about colour theming. The Sheffield School seems to be going even further by suggesting that plants should be selected neither for their form nor colour, but solely on the basis of their ecological suitability (I was going to use the word sustainability, but let's not even go there).

I have to confess that I do have some theoretical problems with the Sheffield School's approach (and not just because I am a 'crazed conceptualist'). The theoretical basis for the creation of 'nature-like vegetation', as it is called, with academic monographs and books replete with graphs and a special new jargon, seeks to create a parity with scientific experimentation (this is an academic department, after all). But the science is simply a front in practical and commercial terms, because what the Sheffield School is really selling is that good old idealization of nature which has been a theme that has loomed large in British culture at least as far back as 'Capability' Brown's national pastoral makeover in the late eighteenth century. Of course what the Sheffield School proposes is just as artificial as any Chaumont installation, yet its chosen terminology – liberal use of words such as 'ecological', 'naturalistic' and 'sustainable' – means that the idea of the 'made' in design remains unacknowledged and is perhaps even played down for commercially expedient reasons (because we all know that eco sells at the moment, while 'garden design' is still popularly associated with the woeful excesses of Alan Titchmarsh and Diarmuid Gavin).

It also worries me that the basic social message of the Sheffield School – that it is a good idea to put a field in the middle of a city – is inappropriate in most contemporary urban contexts. Philosophically, why can't we face up to the fact that most people live in cities, not the countryside? Practically speaking, where can kids play football? And in terms of aesthetics, have we just given up on design, subscribing instead to that lame old cliché: 'nature is the best designer'? That amounts to an admission of the failure of design. Do we agree with that? Wake up and smell the compost!

Garden Design Journal

WHAT A WAY TO GO
AUGUST 2009
↬

WHAT A WAY TO GO! Or nearly go.

There I was, innocently, some would say insouciantly, sipping a glass of pink champagne on the pavement outside a hotel just over from Green Park, while munching on slightly incongruous canapés in the form of tiny morsels of chocolate and fruitcake as proferred by several waves of chic, brown-uniformed waitresses – somewhat to the bemusement it must be said of Piccadilly's passers-by, who, you would have thought, would have been used to over-the-top behaviour like street champagne parties – when suddenly there was an almighty 'Carrumph' beside me, followed by peals of amazed laughter from various assembled garden hacks.

Looking down, I noticed lying on the ground what I first took to be a small rhododendron but which was, it transpired, an unusual form of viburnum, though I cannot now recall the species name (quite understandably in the circumstances). The plant had been blown out of its socket, in high winds, from some sixty feet up the new living wall which Patrick Blanc has planted across one entire corner of the facade of the Athenaeum Hotel. It had landed right next to me. If it had hit me it would probably not have finished me off (a shame, some may say, regretting the 'Killed by a Living Wall' headline) but it might well have knocked me down, especially considering the champagne aspect of the equation. In which case I would be the first ever writer in the history of horticultural journalism to be able, legitimately, to use the word 'stunning' to describe a plant.

My first reaction to this unusual happening was, in the English way, embarrassment. I felt it was somehow my fault. I had messed up the grand opening of Monsieur Blanc's new living wall by nearly being hit by one of his plants travelling earthwards at 60 mph. So I immediately put down my champagne glass, picked up the viburnum and urgently tried to engineer a home for it in one of the planting boxes hanging on the railings by the hotel. But it was too late. Monsieur Blanc (he of the tropical shirts and green hair) had been alerted by the shrill journos and wafted up with a look of concern on his face.

'What 'az 'appened?' he asked. 'What? Er, nothing...' I stammered, feeling as if I had been caught bunking off games. 'There it is! There it is!' catcalled my colleagues, pointing to the badly planted viburnum in the planter. While Monsieur Blanc grubbed about in the soil he explained that this really was a very unusual occurrence, while I assured him that nearly being brained by a shrub is just one of those things which happens in the life of a busy garden writer.

That is not strictly true, of course, especially in this health-and-safety conscious country, though in America last year I had close shaves with both alligators and killer bees in gardens. Professional gardeners are probably in more peril, clipping topiary in precarious positions, for example (I recall the head gardener at the Huntington Desert Garden in California telling me that members of his staff have had to be physically cut out from the spiny arms of large cacti before now).

The point of all this is that, despite everything, I really admire Monsieur Blanc's new living wall – and all the other ones he has made (though not all of those by his emulators).

If a designer has one really good, original idea, it seems to me that it does not matter if they simply go on developing it during their career, *pace* Jencks and landforms, Dreiseitl and water tricks, Oudolf and perennials, or Schwartz and conceptualism. Very often this idea is something which occurred to them early on – even in childhood (Blanc began messing about with vertical planting when he was fourteen). Newer designers might take note that one really good technical or material innovation can make an international career. Just don't ask me what that idea might be. And don't throw it at me.

Garden Design Journal

RHS JUDGING
OCTOBER 2009
ᴥ

A RECENT 'DEBATE' (ambush) about Royal Horticultural Society judging standards, held at the Hampton Court Flower Show, prompted by a stray paragraph in this very column, was a regrettably fractious affair (you can follow developments online if you google 'sparks fly' and my name).

My intention was to point up systemic shortcomings in the RHS system in order to help improve matters for designers, the public and garden making as a whole. I stand by my basic point, that the RHS monopoly on award giving is all too cosy at the moment, while both the judging system and the judging panel are in need of reform. Honestly, judging by the reaction from the RHS you'd think I'd suggested compulsory nude gnomes in every show garden.

One of my reformist ideas is that an international element to the selection and judging of gardens is needed if the RHS really does aspire to make its events into a showcase of international garden design. I was genuinely surprised at the assertion from the RHS's chief show-garden judge Andrew Wilson that Chelsea Flower Show can be considered an international gold standard of garden design, with an RHS gold medal something which designers from foreign climes aim at.

Now I am not here to knock the RHS – Chelsea in particular really does represent the cutting edge in plantsmanship and the show gardens probably are the best in the world, for what they are. But it is simply fantasy to imagine that leading foreign designers see it as in any way relevant to their own careers. It is inconceivable that a Fernando Caruncho or a Vladimir Djuvoric would initiate or solicit a Chelsea show garden. The RHS claims it has strong links with international designers, but there is little evidence of this. Admittedly Ulf Nordfjell from Sweden 'won' this year, but he has long had unusually strong links with Britain and just missed out a few years ago. He has played the game. Andrew says: 'Whilst there are many designers across the world for whom I have the greatest respect, the majority have little or no experience in designing and building show gardens.' Poor them! No Chelsea, then, for the likes of Caruncho, Djuvoric or Dan Hinkley. Can't the RHS help them?

On the judging side, the argument from the RHS that show gardens are assessed, ideally, only by those who have experience of those same shows is surely a contributing factor to the sense of an 'RHS bubble' of show gardens which so many people complain about. It's not about whether the judges have got it right or not in the past; it's about how it all looks to the outside world. By any definition the RHS system really is 'cosy' to a freemasonic degree – yet those involved are claiming that insularity of that kind is actually a benefit to us all, even though (poor pets) we don't have the wherewithal to understand that.

Finally, there is the archaic percentile marking system, which is heavily geared towards planting, whatever the judges claim. Of this, Andrew states: 'There are few restrictions on design submissions although it must be borne in mind that the RHS is dedicated to horticulture and its shows are used as vehicles for the development and dissemination of horticultural excellence.'

I am not sure whether Andrew actually wrote that last sentence himself. I'd be surprised if he did – the telltale use of the corporate-speak word 'excellence' gives it away. But there, amidst all the posturing about design, I think we have the RHS's real attitude to garden design encapsulated.

Garden Design Journal

GARDENING CLOTHES
DECEMBER 2009
⤚

ONE OF THE MOST TALKED-ABOUT films of the past year was *Man on Wire*, which chronicled the astonishing exploits of high-wire artist Philippe Petit, who dared to walk along a wire strung between the twin towers of the World Trade Center in New York. I have not yet seen the film but stills of Petit standing on his wire in mid-air between the towers crop up all over the place. What strikes me most forcibly about these images is not the fact he is 'dicing with death', but that he is wearing the most extravagant pair of flared trousers, or 'flares', I have ever seen. This was 1974, after all, and such things are to be expected, but surely such wide flares constituted a safety hazard, what with all those cross-winds? Why was the daredevil not blown off?

Flares were also de rigueur for gardening in the 1970s, to judge by contemporary gardening manuals, in which guys brandish shredders and chippers or hover mowers – 'because it's a lot less bovva with a hover' – and gals wield the secateurs while clad in psychedelic floral blouses which look as if they have been designed by someone who has had one too many swigs of the Baby Bio. These 1970s gardeners always seem to be wearing unisex bright blue denim flares. These are most impractical because they could easily become snagged in moving parts and, as I recall, would become sodden with dew almost immediately if one was gardening in long grass or in a border.

What to wear, or not to to wear, is a vexed question for gardening types, professional and otherwise. Germaine Greer had a gardening column in *Private Eye* in the 1970s for which she used the pseudonym 'Rose Blight'. Here is the opening of one column, entitled 'Voyeurs': 'My mother used to garden semi-naked, with an old pair of knickers wrapped around her hair to keep the dust out. In colder weather, she would rope up a pair of father's old trousers and put on a cardigan back to front. Thus attired, she felt ready for anything.'

Does anyone recognize themselves there? It's a look.

Or you can go the other way, and go all haughty-couture for your horti-culture. Here is New York fashion buyer Dianne Benson ruminating on garden clothes in her 1994 book *Dirt*: 'You do need gardening clothes that are sensible and chic at the same time. My fashion instincts do not leave me even when on my knees on the dampest, coldest, dreariest days of November planting the blackest tulips one can order.' Benson goes on to suggest that Vita Sackville-West got it right with her gardening wardrobe, based on a foundation of riding jodphurs (surely the sartorial antithesis of flares), 'usually topped with a big white man's shirt and either a severe black jacket or an oversize natty cardigan, which could only be English'. Benson also notes approvingly that Vita never took off her pearls simply because she was gardening. Slightly more controversially, Benson confesses to requisitioning her husband's silk underwear one cold day and finding it eminently comfortable and warm. 'Now,' she adds, 'slipping on my own silk underwear at any sign of penetrating damp weather has become almost religious.'

I have only raised the topic of silk underwear because it is the Christmas season and one's loved ones may be enquiring about potential gifts. What do you get the gardener who has everything? It is my sincere hope that garden designers everywhere, both male and female, will be unwrapping parcels of silk underwear – for gardening in – on Christmas Day.

Garden Design Journal

THE POLITICS OF SELF-SUFFICIENCY
DECEMBER 2009
↦

EVERY GARDEN IS A POLITICAL ACT. Every plant is a political prisoner. That statement is not meant to imply that every allotment owner is presiding over some kind of vegetable Guantanamo Bay. There are, however, cultural implications bound up with the apparently beneficent or at least harmless pastime of growing fruit and veg for the table. Whether the gardener feels political or not when feeling under the earth for the first potatoes or fending off slugs with grit and old beer, there can be no doubt that the decision to delve is, at this particular moment of ecological dismay, an act of powerful political piquancy. In fact, as this short essay aims to show, gardening for food is a pastime which has a considerable political pedigree. That is despite the cosy, popular view of gardening as an even more banal cousin of DIY, something to do when one has grown old or failed in life. That patronizing stereotype should be a red rag to the bullish instincts of all those suspicious of the state-prescribed work ethic. For gardening is, to paraphrase Francis Bacon, the most purely idle of human pleasures; it is possible to be as amply rewarded for a very little as for a great deal of work, and – gloriously – there is no sure connection between the amount of energy and effort expended while gardening, and what results from it. You can be a good gardener by doing very little, and a bad gardener by doing too much. The weather and other intangibles constantly undercut the 'virtues' of hard graft. And from a political point of view, the gardener as 'home-worker' is about as far removed from the developed capitalist system as it is possible to be, growing produce for home consumption in a kitchen just a few yards away, and usually donating any surplus food to friends and neighbours for free.

But to get back to the current craze for grow-your-own. Allotments now boast lengthy waiting lists and, to judge from book sales at least, thousands of people from their twenties to forties (most of them women) have taken up horticulture. The influx of these novices has led to considerable bemusement on the part of the traditional, middle-aged, male, marrow-growing constituency out there in shed-land. The motivation among the newcomers is not a sudden urge to grow gigantic vegetables but instead stems from a desire to grow both for flavour and as a way of being quite sure of the provenance of the food on the kitchen table. There is a great deal of mistrust around the food industry as a whole, let alone retail outlets such as supermarkets or the ethics or otherwise of the meat industry. There are growing and sometimes well-founded suspicions, too, about large-scale commercial organic horticulture. As a result, the twenty-first-century grow-your-own movement has a slightly apocalyptic, post-industrial, millennarian savour to it, as if people are hunkering down in preparation for Armageddon. This time, however, it appears the apocalypse is expected to be ecological rather than nuclear in flavour. Better start bottling those plums, then.

In reality, it is only allotments in the most affluent and fashionable areas of cities which are experiencing a surge – elsewhere, allotments are still being closed down for lack of interest. But it could well be the case that these elite (or bourgeois) early-adopters of a low-tech sensibility in a high-tech age are in the vanguard of a wider movement. It would take a brave television chef or gardener to gainsay 'going organic' or cast doubt on the real ecological impact of domestic vegetable growing. Perhaps mass public opinion will follow in their wake.

From the standpoint of garden history, we have been here before: the current high visibility of the grow-your-own phenomenon is reminiscent of the Dig for Victory campaign of the Second World War, only the enemy now is climate change rather than the Nazis. In fact there was a concerted campaign aimed at encouraging domestic veg production during the First World War, too, when allotments first appeared on railway land. But it is the 1940s incarnation of patriotic gardening which still looms large in the national consciousness and that is because Dig for Victory achieved enduring success as a propaganda campaign. As such, it remains as much a part of folk memory of the war as the Battle of Britain.

The truth is, while a (small) proportion of the populace certainly did grow their own for some part of the Second World War, the effect it had on homegrown resources was negligible compared with less exciting innovations such as increased mechanization in agriculture (all those Land Girls driving shiny new tractors) and the reclamation of marshland or other unused hectares for large-scale crop-growing. Even so, despite these measures, during the first years of the war Britain remained dependent on ship-borne supplies of grain from Canada and the USA. Mrs Miggins's back-garden radishes were just not a part of the equation from the Ministry of Food's point of view. Imagine if Britain had been invaded and London had become a second Stalingrad? In that context the Dig for Victory campaign would barely be recalled today. The real message of Dig for Victory, as sent from the Government to the beleaguered populace, lay in the way it fostered a sense that British people of all classes were 'all in this together', with pictures of the lawns of stately homes being ploughed up next to images of cheery cockneys brandishing bunches of carrots. It was good propaganda material for a nation under threat and bombed from the air, but not yet physically invaded. 'Potato Pete' was one of the manically smiling cartoon characters used on posters, bizarrely encouraging people to eat either himself or his tuberous confederates. And perhaps he did cheer people up and make them feel that everything would be all right in the end. One should never underestimate the morale-boosting power of the chip in British life.

The similarities with today's horticultural zeitgeist lie in the way vegetable gardening is effectively being marketed by the politicians and their civilian lackeys as a way of 'making a difference' to the environmental world order, even if the effect of this in a global context is virtually nil. The sense of eco-guilt which politicians seek to imbue in each of us, as if we are all individually culpable in some way for the conundrum of our deteriorating if not dying planet, needs assuaging somehow, and gardening does seem to salve consciences, just as recycling seemed to a decade ago. There is also a class element to this. A relatively high proportion of eco-commentators and activists are upper class or upper middle class. This particular cause appeals to a strong inbred patrician sensibility. Whether or not these activists would feel comfortable acknowledging it, the eco movement re-emphasizes ancient links between land and agriculture and British political and social power; those who feel linked to the landed or gentry classes will often experience a sense of rightness about being involved with land custodianship in some way. On a deeper cultural level, horticulture itself has long been considered an inherently virtuous pastime – think back to that period in the Garden of Eden, before Man's first disobedience. Gardening does indeed tend to make people feel good about themselves, also healthier mentally, physically and perhaps even morally (though that last conflation is surely illusory).

Vegetable gardening can serve, too, as a form of political or cultural protest. The last time Britain experienced a surge in the popularity of self-sufficiency on this scale was in the years following the Middle East oil crisis of 1973, when for the first time there was genuine uncertainty as to whether there would be enough energy to go round. (The answer today is clearly 'no', but it was not as obvious then.) This was the period of the *Whole Earth Catalog* and John Seymour's seminal guide to self-sufficiency, when the idea of alternative lifestyles first gained serious currency. The movement quickly became such a part of mainstream culture that it could be satirized in a television sitcom like *The Good Life* (where, I have to say, I always identified more with Gerry – he of the checked trousers and G&Ts – than with the insufferably smug goody-goody Tom).

The equivocation of food production and political power goes back to the beginnings of organized agriculture in Britain, and is tied up with the facts of land ownership. Until relatively recently there was a direct link between land ownership and political power in that only those who owned a certain acreage could vote, let alone be eligible to become an MP. When the Tory party's traditional hegemony was first threatened by the nascent Whig party in the late seventeenth century, it became desirable for politicians of every stripe to re-emphasize their country credentials by pursuing the latest ideas in estate management. This was really a peculiarly British admixture of the vogue for emulating the Virgilian or Ciceronian concept of the civilized country retreat away from the noise of town, with a down-to-earth appreciation of the inherent virtue and utility of agriculture. It led to a new emphasis on the importance of horticulture and self-sufficiency at estates – increasingly, orchards and kitchen gardens were integrated into the designed landscape, which gradually became more naturalistic when compared with the formal decorative parterres and fountains of the Baroque tradition (associated with Catholic Europe). For a Whig grandee such as the Duke of Newcastle of Claremont in Surrey, who was prime minister twice, gifts of baskets of ripe peaches sent to his political friends and enemies in London served as a way of emphasizing how competent and relaxed he was at his country estate, undercutting Tory jibes that the Whigs were all *nouveaux riches*. At this point the humble apple could become the chief symbolic subject of a patriotic poem such as 'Cyder'(1708) by the Whig propagandist poet John Philips, a sensous evocation of English agriculture which paints a picture of the country in a kind of Edenic state of ripeness:

> . . . whilst English Plains
> Blush with pomaceous Harvests, breathing Sweets.
> O let me now, when the kind early Dew
> Unlocks th' embosom'd Odors, walk among
> The well rang'd Files of Trees, whose full-ag'd Store
> Diffuse Ambrosial Streams.

Fruit was venerated in British culture from the medieval period up to the mid-twentieth century, when it finally became commonplace. Exotic fruit, requiring expensive hothouse production or contact with plant collectors abroad, was a particularly potent status symbol, with the pineapple at the top of the tree – witness the celebrated painting of the King's gardener, John Rose, presenting Charles I with the first pineapple grown in England. Fruit for dessert, and not just exotic hothouse produce such as pineapples or melons, was for centuries considered a delicacy at any English table. Those eighteenth- and nineteenth-century dessert services by Royal Worcester and other English potteries, with individual apple or pear varieties lovingly painted on each plate and bowl, are a reflection of the esteem in which fresh-picked fruit was traditionally held. And it was often paired with cream, of course, another agricultural product which was sentimentally venerated in the literature. In some of England's most extravagant houses today it is still possible to enjoy fruit served as a dessert course in the traditional Victorian aristocratic manner, with fruit bushes or dwarf trees wheeled into the dining room on trolleys so that diners can snip off their own fruit and enjoy that fresh-plucked flavour.

All of that may seem a long way from growing carrots and spuds out back in the hope they might furnish a meal or two. But given that for most people today this is a lifestyle choice rather than an economic or nutritional necessity, the current grow-your-own movement has to be seen as part of the continuum of political gardening in this country.

All of the above is not a cynical attack on the idea of turning a garden over to vegetables. I have done it myself, and am much more content with my own plot as a result. For years I pursued the ideal of creating a kind of miniature Sissinghurst in a succession of London yard gardens, which were originally designed for hanging out washing and housing the lavatory. In a yard garden, a more utilitarian approach feels much more appropriate, though I do still have ornamental plants like roses around the edges of my central plot. Gardening for food in the current 'climate', as it were, feels good because it is a way of asserting oneself in the face of apparently insurmountable ecological odds. So what if it makes little difference to the fate of the planet? There is a lot to be said for veg gardening as a powerful demonstration of personal autonomy and political expression. In that sense, it can be seen as a benign yet eminently useful form of direct action – and the so-called 'guerilla gardeners', who go out at night and garden dismal public spaces, ought to be mentioned in this context. This is going to sound pretentious to some, but perhaps the garden might be understood as the arena where we act out the drama of our relationship with nature on a personal, domestic level. It's a physical relationship, too, an authentic expression of 'being in the world', to stray into Heideggerian phenomenology for a moment.

Every garden is indeed a political act. Every plant is indeed a political prisoner. Which makes every gardener a tyrant. But each of us, in our own private realm, can at least rehearse the kind of tyranny over which we wish to preside.

The Idler

SERRE DE LA MADONE
JANUARY 2010
↭

THE REDISCOVERY AND RESTORATION of Serre de la Madone, Lawrence Johnston's 'other' garden (he also owned Hidcote) just outside Menton on the French Riviera, is surely one of the most exciting stories in the world of gardens today. Overgrown and neglected through the 1980s, over the past decade the garden has been stripped down and then built up again so that it can be appreciated once more as a true masterpiece of garden design, arguably as distinguished as Hidcote itself. Today the garden is under state control (the Conservatoire du Littoral) and the integrity of Johnston's original structural design can be appreciated to the full.

Johnston came to the Riviera in 1924. He chose a property in the Gorbio Valley west of Menton because of the delightfully isolated and sequestered atmosphere that still persists today. The bachelor Johnston' s annual routine until the Second World War involved driving down from England in October and staying until mid-April. Catering to his needs at Serre he had a staff of twenty-three, including twelve gardeners. Johnston was deeply immersed in plant-hunting expeditions in the 1920s and his Riviera garden provided a suitable climate for many of the more tender species sourced from places such as China and Mexico. His companions on these trips were famous collectors including E. A. Bowles, 'Cherry' Ingram and George Forrest, though Forrest for one was unimpressed by Johnston's 'gadding about' in China, while the more congenial Ingram felt it was a bit over-the-top of him to bring a chauffeur and butler/cook along on an expedition. But as at Hidcote, Serre was not just a depository for thousands of botanical specimens selected by a discerning owner. Its *raison d'être* was just as much aesthetic, and Johnston organized the plants with a flair that was widely admired, patrolling the garden each day with a veritable pack of dogs in his wake (seven dachshunds, two Pyrenean mountain dogs and a bull mastiff).

All modern descriptions of the garden begin at the foot of its terraces and work upwards, since this is where the modern visitor arrives. But that is not how Johnston planned it. Let us imagine we are his guests and experience the garden as he meant us to.

Our chauffeur deposits us halfway up the garden's terraces, behind the orangery. Passing through its exotic delights we emerge into the broad light of the garden's main terrace, dignified by a large rectangular pool that is shaded by massive pines and adorned by eight green-glazed pots. At the far end of this terrace is another, smaller pool filled with lotuses surrounding a statue of Venus. This is a glamorous and luxurious space, a fitting prelude to luncheon in the ochre-painted house six terraces above, which will be served by waiters in tails.

A central flight of steps takes visitors up the terraces. Each level is adorned with a simple fountain, in a nod to Italian Renaissance tradition that also makes a decorative virtue of the necessity of irrigation. Behind the house looms a large area of woodland, which in Johnston's time contained a big netted aviary.

Two rectangular terraces, one paved, the other adorned by a 'Moroccan' pool, extend across the terraces by the house, both taking the visitor to a circular belvedere with plunging diagonal views across the garden, down to the orangery terrace and beyond to a plat consisting of four plane trees underplanted with box hedges, tulips and vinca. This belvedere and its vista can be understood as the key moment of the garden: its circular form strikes a new note in a garden where the aesthetic is defined generally by the narrowness and length of its multiple terraces. From the water garden halfway up, the lower terraces are hidden from view and are thereby made more mysterious. A narrow, curving pergola spans the garden and marks this point of transition.

One suspects that in Johnston's day the lower terraces were the preserve of the horticulturally interested, and today successful attempts are being made at reinstating collections of Mexican, South African and Antipodean plants. There is a new salvia terrace, aster beds, an exciting protea terrace, a corner for rush-like restios, a camellia collection and a general emphasis on scented shrubs such as viburnum, abelia, lonicera and sarcococca, together with unusual trees, including *Cocculus laurifolius* from Japan. Mexican succulents, agaves and opuntia are left to mingle with maquis herbs such as lavender, rosemary and oregano, as they were in the 1930s. A fine specimen of *Mahonia siamensis* (with long yellow racemes) survives: it was brought back by Johnston from Yunnan in 1931 and introduced to cultivation by him. Rough winding paths show the way to the lowest part of the garden, where another, much smaller hothouse (now roofless) is hidden away. Adorned by religious statuary, it has something of the character of a woodland shrine – Johnston was a religious man, and the 'Madone' in the garden's name refers to the Madonna. It's a quiet, contemplative spot in a garden that attracts relatively few visitors despite its pedigree. An old *Magnolia delavayi* from Johnston's time still stands just here, making as fine an end to a truly classic garden as it does a beginning.

Gardens Illustrated

GHOSTS
JANUARY 2010
↔

GARDENS CAN BE such atmospheric, mysterious places that it seems surprising that the very first book on the subject of ghosts in gardens should have appeared, or manifested itself, just a few months ago. Peter Underwood, author of *Haunted Gardens*, is a serial ghost author, compiler of a gazetteer to Britain's spooks and president of the Ghost Club Society.

The thirty or so case studies in the book, covering gardens such as Chenies Manor and Jenkyn Place, are filled with all the usual nonsense about grey ladies and headless courtiers, presumably designed to provoke a pleasurable frisson in the credulous, the gullible, the suggestible and the susceptible. We are told, for example, that the lakeside at Charlecote Park is haunted by the figure of a 'mysterious' girl in white, who is believed to have drowned herself there. Then it is dropped in that Shakespeare is said to have written Ophelia's death scene at the house. Coincidence? Maybe . . .

Wait a minute. If one stops to think about it, the haunting is obviously a total fabrication, the ghost story simply extrapolated from an unlikely, though appealing, family Shakespeare legend.

Perhaps I am being a little over-harsh because I am in fact drawn to this subject. Not because I 'believe' in ghosts and apparitions of the type evoked in ghost stories, but because there is an affinity, which may only be metaphorical, between the idea of ghosts in gardens and the classical notion of spirit of place – the *genius loci*, as Alexander Pope famously dubbed it. Sometimes the atmosphere in a garden can be so strong that it is tempting to follow classical precedent and think of it as being an independent entity of some kind.

One can certainly get a sense of this looking at old photographs of gardens – the Edwardian images in *Country Life*'s archive are perhaps the best example. Looming yew hedges, crumbling staircases, still pools and even the occasional figure dressed all in white drifting by – images such as this conspire to create a strong sense of atmosphere which can seem not a little ghostly. But of course these photographs, like so many good ghost stories, are carefully constructed fabrications.

A few years ago I found myself formulating a theory of sense of place called 'psychotopia', which posits the existence of a kind of mind or 'psyche' (if only a set of memories) belonging to a 'topos' or place. It proved relatively uncontroversial: professional garden designers and landscape architects were happy to acknowledge that identifying and then manipulating an existing *genius loci* is their bread and butter, just as it was for Pope. But of course, instinctive belief in such a process is not 'rational' in the empirical, scientific sense.

The key to this is the conviction that the people who own, visit or simply pass through gardens and landscapes become co-creators of the sense of place, leaving behind invisible yet tangible impressions of their interactions with it. These psychic alterations may be so small as to be imperceptible (someone visiting a garden for a single afternoon, perhaps) or they may be decisive (a keen gardener in their own garden – and who would argue that their character will not somehow be bound up in the place?)

Following up on this, I was keen to find out whether the Lost Gardens of Heligan featured in *Haunted Gardens*. That is the one garden where I have personally encountered ex-gardeners who say they have felt uneasy if not downright terrified at certain times and in certain areas of the garden. The rockery and fruit store are usually singled out as hot spots: people prefer to work in pairs in these areas. One of the gardeners I spoke to told me he simply refused to lock up the garden at night on his own.

Interviewing Tim Smit at Heligan some fifteen years ago, I remember asking him about the garden's ghosts in a light way. I was surprised at how serious he became, confirming several stories I had heard and adding some of his own, and then asking me not to print any reference to what he had said. Several years later, in his own memoir of the garden, Tim finally revealed just how difficult matters had become from a managerial point of view at that time, with members of staff deeply disturbed and apparently beset by an enveloping black mood. Exorcisms had ensued.

It seems to me that in some cases 'hauntings' are the result of some form of mass, or perhaps more precisely communal, hysteria. That may be what happened at Heligan among a close-knit gardens team, often working alone, surrounded by stories of the garden's past. On the other hand, there is no denying that Heligan is an extremely atmospheric place. It may be that the existing 'space-flavour' of the garden was enhanced or unearthed by the sudden presence of an army of restorers. Perhaps the garden's 'ghosts', or more accurately its innate characteristics, were revealed again just as the tree ferns in the combe also began to see the light of day after a century and more in obscurity.

Country Life

LANDFORM
APRIL 2010
↔

AT THE MOST CUTTING EDGE of landscaping among go-ahead private owners just now is landforming or turf sculpture. The idea is simple: beautiful flowing berms of turf shaped into curves, swirls, steps or gentle slopes, often offset by arc-shaped pools of water or still, black ponds. It is a surprisingly versatile look which can be made to appear formal or abstract, achievable on a large-scale or in a relatively modest acreage, though it must be said that this is not an option for the townhouse in Putney.

The subtle pleasure of landform lies in the play of light and shadow on the green grass, not just during the passage of the seasons but even across the trajectory of a single day. Imagine waking up at dawn to look out of the window and watch the indistinct blue-grey forms of a turf sculpture gradually take on life as the sun's rays reach it. Droplets of dew catch the rays and twinkle like thousands of tiny spotlights, before the sun starts to light up the chlorophyll in the grass and the whole scene begins to warm up and glow. Frost will have a magical effect, of course, but an August dusk can be equally beguiling, as the sharp edges of the grassed forms start to melt away, melding with each other as day dissolves into night. And even in the uncompromisingly strong light of midday, when shapes and colours alike tend to be flattened, landforms have a trick to play in that many and various shadows come alive, creating intriguingly intense patterns on the green canvas.

Landform has been with us in Britain for millennia. Think of neolithic sites or ancient fortifications such as Maiden Castle, with its rings of earthern ramparts. Then there is the medieval tradition of ridge-and-furrow agriculture, which has produced a distinctive wavy landscape in many parts of Britain's countryside. The medieval and Tudor period saw a vogue for mounts in gardens (there is still a fine one in the garden of New College, Oxford, for example) and in the eighteenth century a craze emerged for formal amphitheatres, such as the one at Claremont in Surrey. For centuries British gardeners were renowned for their skill with grass, deployed to best advantage in the bowling greens which were de rigueur in British gardens in the first half of the eighteenth century; the French even deigned to copy the style – dubbing them 'boulingrins'. Then 'Capability' Brown came along and made extensive landforming for picturesque, naturalistic effect the must-have accoutrement for landowners. Of course the humble lawn still has a central place in the gardening culture of this country, either the bane or the pride of (usually male) gardeners' lives.

In the mid-nineties, however, the resilient cult of landform was given a fillip through the example of the American architectural historian Charles Jencks (usually tagged as 'the inventor of post-Modernism'). Inspired by the landscaping experiments of his wife Maggie Keswick, an expert on Chinese landscape history and the 'bones of the earth' traditions of feng-shui, Jencks brought in the bulldozers to devise an astonishing landform garden at their estate in Dumfriesshire. The intellectual basis was an amalgam of all the latest theories surrounding cosmology, in that the central feature of the space, a magnificent S-shaped grass berm offset by pools, was intended to mimic the form of the fractal, or the fractional dimension which exists between the dimensions, representing pure energy. Whether or not one understood all of the scientific underpinnings of this garden (and most did not), the sheer tactile pleasure of walking these mounds, or just gasping at the other-worldly scene, made it one of the most notable gardens to be made in the closing decades of the twentieth century.

It took a while for Jencks's influence to percolate, for the style seemed so much his own. But in the new century a number of others have made landform a key element of their visual vocabulary. In some cases it has just been a matter of empty fashion, but the best designers are by no means mere Jencks copyists and have made an attitude towards landforming very much a part of their own sensibility.

Kim Wilkie is one such. He has just completed an astonishing artwork-landform, entitled 'Orpheus', for the Duke of Buccleuch at Boughton House in Northamptonshire. This is basically a geometrically designed hole in the ground, with a shallow grass path leading down into the bottom of the space, a square black pool. It was designed to complement an existing eighteenth-century mound on the opposite side of a canal in Boughton's extensive formal landscape, and has an extremely strong presence in context. 'Each of my landforms is responding to the site and saying something specific,' Wilkie says. 'You can't just do it for the sake of it – there has to be a clear rationale.'

Wilkie began his experiments with landform in earnest more than a decade ago at Heveningham Hall in Norfolk, where he created an amphitheatre of grass berms for private clients, replacing a rather dull Victorian scheme immediately behind the house. 'I love working with shadow and mist and the times of day and year,' he says. 'It's nice when something can look quite flat and then come alive at a special moment.' Often, he says, he can take advantage of the way large country houses have been built in the lee of a slope (usually to the north), thereby creating a natural rise which can be exploited with terracing.

Wilkie has completed half a dozen such schemes and is now working on several more. These range from a relatively formal landform in the shape of a knot for private clients in Hampshire, to a subtle scheme of low landforming designed to rejuvenate a water meadow at another private house. And in the garden of his own country retreat in Hampshire Wilkie proves that a large acreage is not always necessary for an effective landform: in this case he has shaped a small mound inspired by the hillocks along the edge of the Thames.

Dan Pearson is another notable designer who has worked in the medium of landform in recent years. 'It's a comparatively cheap way of creating space and it doesn't leave a huge ecological footprint – future generations can leave it or change it quite easily,' he says. Like Wilkie, Pearson is adamant that there has to be a practical reason for landforming and strong conceptual thought behind it: 'I've seen quite a lot of misused and misguided landform. There is work out there in this vein and you think, "Why?"'

Done well, Pearson believes turf sculpture to be a particularly suitable medium in this country. 'In the USA they tend to landform in the desert landscape,' he explains, 'but the beauty here is the possibility of softness – it can become voluptuous and tactile.' He is currently working on a landscape for a private estate on the coast of Lincolnshire, where a new house will be offset by a two-acre lake, the spoil from which he will use to create a landform that mimics the patterns sand makes on the seabed just offshore.

Pearson's biggest foray into landform – perhaps the biggest anywhere – is still under way in Japan, where he is masterminding the creation of the Tokachi Millennium Forest, an ecological park on the island of Hokkaido. The landforming was partly a way of solving a problem. 'Visitors arrive at the base of a mountain,' Pearson explains, 'in this huge, undefined space, like standing in the middle of a football pitch where you can't see the edges. I wanted to create an enticement for visitors to walk through the space and up the mountain.' Pearson says he is delighted that it is children who are enthusiastically leading the way. There have been some unexpected benefits, too. 'It's remarkable how the acoustic changes when you are among the landforms, and also the way the mountains feel pulled towards you,' Pearson says.

So what does Charles Jencks himself make of it all? Over lapsang souchong and shards of chocolate at his London townhouse, he is characteristically generous towards those who have become as beguiled as he is by green landforms. But he too is adamant that the aesthetic imperative is not enough on its own. 'All of my work is content-driven,' he says – something of an understatement, given the complexity and detail embedded in his designs. Archaeology is now as much of a preoccupation for Jencks as cosmology. 'Did you know that there are a thousand stone circles in Britain?' he queries. 'No one knows that!' He says he has visited forty or fifty such sites over the past twenty years, a preoccupation with prehistory which adds a valuable emotional or even spiritual dimension to his work.

Jencks's most recent major landform, still unfinished, is Life Mounds, a design based on the structure of cells that is situated on either side of the main drive to Bonnington House in Scotland. Here, owners Robert and Nicky Wilson have commissioned site-specific sculptural works by artists including Anthony Gormley and Andy Goldsworthy and rechristened the estate Jupiter Artland. They opened to the public for the first time last year.

As a 'client' (though in reality, as a sculptor herself, she has played an active creative role in the project), Nicky Wilson professes delight at the reality of 'living with a landform'. 'What is nice about it is we don't have to make a pilgrimage to view the art,' she explains. 'We drive through it and interact with it four or five times a day.' She has been especially gratified by the way sixth-form students and even quite young children have used the landform as a way of understanding how cell structure and cell division works, in some cases tracing the shapes of the forms with a GPS device and mapping it again back in the classroom. On the other hand she describes the landform as a visually soothing experience – 'It's a very beautiful thing to live with. It's soothing because I know that it has been considered very carefully and that all the lines are true and right. We're very proud of it, really.'

And so to practicalities. Kim Wilkie has his colleagues map 'down to the last millimetre' the positioning of his turf features, and he praises the 'incredibly skilful' digger drivers they work with. 'For Orpheus,' he says, 'I would say there is only one digger driver in Britain who could have done it.' Dan Pearson usually makes a plasticine model for the digger driver, 'because it's so much more tangible than a plan on paper'. Jencks works in the same way. As for maintenance, these turf mounds only need mowing, but they must be kept pristine. Any bare patches in the grass or sagging of mounds can ruin the look. Nicky Wilson says they have one man mowing the landform two days per week in summer (which adds up). Pearson acknowledges that the high level of maintenance can be a drawback. 'We've done one tiny landform, just five metres across, in a walled garden for a client, and I think it's become a bit of a burden for him because it needs to be perfect.'

On the other hand, perhaps we would be crazy not to exploit a medium so suited to the British climate, with its fairly reliably wet summers and quick rejuvenation of grass. Dan Pearson puts it succinctly: 'We can do it here because the grass stays green.'

Financial Times

CHANTICLEER MEETS GREAT DIXTER
MAY 2010
⊷

WE ARE WELL USED TO THE IDEA of towns twinning with foreign counterparts, but what about gardens? One example is the partnership between Hidcote and Serre de la Madone on the French Riviera, both gardens made by Lawrence Johnston in the early twentieth century. In this case it seems fitting that an exchange scheme for gardeners (and plants) has been set up, since just such a symbiotic relationship existed in Johnston's day. There are also, of course, plenty of historical links between international gardens owned by individuals or by branches of the same family, such as the Rothschilds.

But what about gardens which have hitherto had no familial relationship, but which somehow seem complementary? Could this sort of interchange prove fruitful? It's a creatively stimulating idea, so it may not come as a surprise to hear that the gardens involved in a pioneer scheme along these lines are Chanticleer in Pennsylvania and our own Great Dixter, two of the most exciting and independent horticultural set-ups in the world.

Dixter will be familiar, but Chanticleer is perhaps not yet as well known as it should be. Situated in the small town of Wayne, just outside Philadelphia, until twenty years ago this was a good if not exceptional country garden created in the early twentieth century by the Rosengarten family, a chemicals manufacturing dynasty.

The attractively undulating 32-acre estate consists of sweeping lawns, areas of woodland, a meandering stream and enclosed formal spaces around an attractive, mansard-roofed house. When Adolph Rosengarten Junior died in 1990 he left Chanticleer in the care of a trust, with few stipulations other than that it be preserved as open space. The board of trustees (including several members of the Rosengarten family) found they had a free hand to develop the place as they wished, and it was at this point that everything changed.

An exuberant new British garden director, Chris Woods, was appointed and he immediately put into place an exceptionally enlightened if high-risk horticultural regime which is still pursued today under director Bill Thomas. Eight head gardeners – who are all equal in the hierarchy – have each been given their own area of the estate to develop as they wish. One of them has the formal spaces ranged across the shallow terraces around the house, another has the wooded stream garden and pond garden, another the Asian Woods, another The Ruin, an estate house deliberately part-demolished to create a folly environment.

The tone of each area reflects the personality and style of the gardener charged with looking after them. Perhaps predictably, given the opportunities for self-expression, Chanticleer has attracted and retained a remarkably diverse collection of powerful characters, who are all happy to chat with visitors in that appealingly unbuttoned American way. Every garden has its theatrical side, but at Chanticleer that sense of 'show-time' approaching becomes palpable in the weeks before opening day each spring.

One of the most theatrical spaces is a former tennis court near the garden entrance which has been transformed into a sunken garden of five rectangular beds. Here one can delight in strident plantings such as prickly purple *Berberis* 'Rose Glow' alternated with the vivid greens and yellows of dwarf bamboo *Pleioblastus variegatus* (for once the Latin seems apt, for 'blast us' is exactly what this colour combination seems to do). If this is not enough, the golden foliage of *Spiraea thunbergii* 'Ogon' combines with the yellow spikes of *Yucca flaccida* 'Golden Sword' and the purple fronds of phormiums. As at Dixter, this is not so much unfettered Edwardiana as something akin to deranged Victoriana.

The director will intervene or advise where necessary, and there are constant passionate discussions between the eight gardeners – which I enjoyed while staying at Chanticleer for a few days this spring – but essentially the horticulturists have a special dispensation to do as they wish. Not every idea works, but the spirit of experimentation can always be admired. Who wants to visit a garden for 'more of the same', anyway? The result is a garden bursting with new ideas, energy, unexpected beauty and sheer fun.

All of those epithets can be applied to Great Dixter, both in Christopher Lloyd's time and equally now it is in the care of Fergus Garrett. So the partnership seems a perfect fit. This year three gardeners from Pennsylvania are spending time in Sussex, while Dixter's own assistant head gardener, Tom Coward, will go to Chanticleer for a month, living on the estate. Fergus Garrett sees the partnership as a way of nurturing a new generation of gardeners, while Bill Thomas says he hopes his staff will return from Britain 'creatively reinvigorated' – and one can hardly imagine how that will not be the case.

Country Life

'REAL' GARDENING?
SEPTEMBER 2010
⊷

NEVER UNDERESTIMATE the passionate disdain with which 'real gardeners' decry the idea of design in gardens. This was forcibly brought home to me yet again recently when I found myself in hot dispute with another garden writer who angrily claimed that garden design was a waste of time, an irrelevance to ordinary gardeners, a realm of pure pretension, wilful waffle. If she had her way, there would be a show garden at Chelsea entitled 'My Garden' which would feature dead and dying plants, evidence of neglect, hosepipes, green-plastic watering cans and other detritus redolent of horticultural life as it is actually lived.

Andy Sturgeon's gorgeous bronze irises in terracotta pots at Chelsea this year came in for particular scorn, on the grounds that visitors to the show would be unaware that any single-flower display of this type will necessarily be short-lived and soon need replacing.

Apparently this sort of thing is irresponsible, misleading and ought to be stopped.

Does this garden writer have a point? Well, no. It seems to me to be patronizing in the extreme to suppose that 'real gardeners' might want to go to a garden show to see mirror images of their own plots, as opposed to fantastical extravaganzas or new ideas. As for Sturgeon's irises, surely every single gardener (and non-gardener) on the planet is aware that flowers die.

So where does this venom come from? The anti-design agenda of some parts of the horticultural world is in part based on a shires-gentry brand of anti-intellectualism which sees design, and talk of design, as essentially vulgar. The country-garden conceit is that you just throw it all together and then, as a result of genetics or feudalism or something, it happens to look good. Women gardeners are particularly susceptible to this kind of snobbery, since ladies of the manor – the Vitas, Rosemarys and Penelopes of this world – have become horticultural role models (not their fault). Even the late, great Christopher Lloyd went in for such disingenous piffle – the argument being that the 'design' (hedge system) he inherited at Great Dixter meant he was never 'a designer' and did not have to think spatially. Er, right.

Anyway, back to my barney. How amusing it was the next day when I saw the very same garden writer performing in a question-and-answer session about 'better borders' at a garden show. There was a certain amount of discussion around soil preparation and mulching (which reinforced my view that just as weekend personal finance supplements in newspapers ought to be boiled down to two words, 'Buy Property', so horticultural supplements might be replaced with the single word, 'Mulch'). The remaining 80 per cent of the discussion time, however, was devoted to abstruse topics such as colour theming, the use of verticals (especially white) in the border, spatial organization, rhythm, massing and foliage contrast. I don't know what this garden writer thought was under discussion, but it sure sounded like design to me, and design couched at a high aesthetic level, at that. The self-delusion of some of these 'real gardeners' is breathtaking.

It's true, of course, that the average British gardener does not like to acknowledge that what they are doing as a hobby might be considered by some to be a vernacular art form (as the French have cooking, so we have gardening). And it's true that gardening is, to an extent, a technical subject, and that planting design is just one element of garden design. But I do find it curious that so many serious horticulturists should be quite so antagonistic and aggressive about garden design as a topic.

On our side of the fence (or galvanized sound-wall), I've never heard anyone from the design world suggest that 'design-less' gardening is utterly risible, that horticulture is not worthwhile in its own right. The strongest criticism one might hear is that 'plantsmen's gardens' are often a bit trainspotterish and 'spotty'. But designers don't say they should be banned, or that they are a waste of space, or an affront to their own work. 'Real gardeners', on the other hand, often seem to fear that the very existence of garden design threatens their own plot in some way. It's probably bound up with the extraordinarily strong emotional bond some people feel they have with their gardens, which can be as intense, if not more so, than their relationships with human beings.

Perhaps some of these down-to-earth types ought to take a step back and learn to live and let live a bit more. If they're not interested in design (or like to believe they're not), that's fine, but why try to spoil the party for the rest of us? I've got this to say to 'real gardeners': Chill Out!

Garden Design Journal

ROBIN LANE FOX IN OXFORD
SEPTEMBER 2010

⟡

FOR THE PAST FORTY YEARS Robin Lane Fox has quietly nurtured a devoted readership by means of his weekly column in the *Financial Times*, where his forthright opinions are delivered with devil-may-care panache.

At the moment, Robin is chiselling away at the perceived pomposity of the New Perennials movement, dubbing the style 'waving Euro-grasses', while a few decades ago he even got into a skirmish with rival columnist 'Christo' Lloyd (who started it).

Horticulture is not Robin's day job, however: since 1977 he has been fellow in ancient history at New College, Oxford, where we meet on a sunny summer's day in a quadrangle beside a big chestnut-leaved oak – planted by Robin, like most of the plant life on view. So is gardening just a sideline? After all, he has his Hollywood career to think about: Alexander the Great is one of his specialisms and it was in this capacity he acted as adviser to director Oliver Stone during the making of the 2004 epic *Alexander*, even going so far as to appear on horseback in the battle scenes. But Robin says that gardening is essential. 'Without the gardening I would never have been an academic,' he says, or the 'fellow in charge' of the gardens at New College. Indeed, he conducts a tour of the gardens like some exceptionally quick-witted lord of the manor surveying his demesne.

Like many plantsmen, Robin does not believe in garden design (only 'gardening', considered a completely different activity), and the long mixed border at New College fully bears out this approach, with its regular arrangement of key perennials – notably bright white nicotiana and red dahlias – spaced out evenly along its length, like cones on a motorway. Closer up, there is much for plants enthusiasts to enjoy, including a trio of rambler roses against the rear wall named after the classical graces: 'Thalia', 'Euphrosyne' and 'Aglaia'.

87

Robin describes these as 'a retort to my colleagues who wanted to elect token women to honorary fellowships at the college'.

Back in the senior common room. we are soon tucking in to a lunch of chicken curry, profiteroles and rosé. 'I was always a cultivator,' Robin says, 'and that's what I admire, the people who grow. If you don't do it, you're just a voyeur.' Robin was a gardener from a young age and by his teens he was buying mail order plants from the famous Six Hills Nursery – 'One and seven each,' he recalls. 'I remember a climactic outing to Hidcote in 1963 [when he was sixteen] which opened my eyes. I realized what a garden could be. I also went to Waterperry Gardens, where I was blessed by Miss Havergal [principal of the ladies' School of Horticulture]. She asked me to hold a trowel, and when I did so correctly she asked me to choose a plant. For some reason I chose *Arenaria montana*.'

On leaving Eton and before going up to Oxford, Robin applied to Munich Botanic Garden, on the advice of Valerie Finnis, the great alpinist (and networker). 'I was hired by mistake,' Robin claims. 'Our house was called Middleton and they apparently thought I was connected to E.A. Bowles of Myddelton House [another great alpinist].' Later he also worked for a month with the influential cottage gardener Margery Fish at East Lambrook Manor in Somerset.

The greatest influence on Robin was that Anglo-American stylist Nancy Lancaster – he lived for a while in a rented cottage on her estate and they gardened alongside each other. 'Fashion is for people with no taste' is a typical Nancy saying, quoted approvingly by Robin in his new collection of provocative garden essays, *Thoughtful Gardening*. Perhaps inspired by this, Robin says, 'The more I have come to know, the more I've come to believe that there is no clear distinction between good and bad taste.'

After lunch Robin suddenly speculates about a potential other life. 'In the nineteenth century I would have been a vicar,' he says, 'a very useful vicar who would have studied Greek, recorded the local flora and believed in my church building more than in God.' It seems surprising that Robin the Oxford don should be fantasizing about being a Victorian vicar as a delightful anachronism when just across the room is a wooden contraption, clearly still in use, which he tells me was designed specifically to facilitate the passing of port across the hearth without the fellows having to rise from their easy chairs. While Robin is certainly not stuck in the past, this is one of those 'only in Oxford' moments – and long may they linger. However the bottle is transported, there will be many who will wish to raise a glass to another forty years of Robin Lane Fox as a garden columnist.

Gardens Illustrated

IMMERSIVE NOT PICTORIAL
OCTOBER 2010
↩

STRANGE AND EXCITING THINGS are afoot in our herbaceous borders. The New Perennials movement has not come along as advertised and simply taken over British garden style. There has not been a 'Dutch invasion' and few English country house gardens bear much resemblance to Munich's Westpark (Waltham Place being the exception). But the look – or perhaps creed is more accurate – has nevertheless had a substantial effect on many gardens, especially on the work of garden designers keen to stay ahead of the curve.

The net result is that the direction of British planting style has changed. Until the mid-1990s the traditional Arts and Crafts approach to border design prevailed – that is, the idea of the colour-themed border as bequeathed by St Gertrude, or else the amiable 'cottage muddle' envisaged by Margery Fish and promoted by the likes of Vita Sackville-West (or Mrs Nicolson, as Daisy Lloyd always called her). This is still the garden style of choice for the majority of Britons, and it unfurls itself magnificently each year in many of the private gardens open under the *Yellow Book* scheme. But for professionals and switched-on amateurs, by the close of the century this look was becoming dated and untenable both aesthetically and ecologically – though the latter is a big debating point itself.

The ideas of Piet Oudolf and others which were filtering in to this country gave British garden designers the confidence to shelve the books on 'colour-theming' the border and embrace instead the concept of brown and black late-autumn disintegration as a worthwhile aesthetic. That's putting it a little baldly, but among the physical differences we can see appearing during the past decade are the increased use of grasses (of course) as well as certain key perennials, especially the umbellifers. Insistent repetition of identical plants, or of similar forms, now vies with leaf and flower colour as a linking device. Shrubs have in many cases been replaced by large grasses or substantal clumps of tall perennials, much to the chagrin of traditional plantsmen like Roy Lancaster. And generally in gardens one can detect a decline in the idea that the herbaceous border should be the showpiece and highlight of any garden; instead, the tone of the planting is extended across the garden's spaces in a less hierarchical manner.

Those who say that this is simply a reprise of William Robinson's nineteenth-century wild gardening are mistaken. For Robinson, the 'pictorial' view, at the middle or long range, was still most important, while any exotica could be introduced so long as they could grow happily. Among today's wild gardeners, obviously 'exotic' flora is excised in favour of subjects which 'could' – conceivably – be native to the region (though very often they are not), while in terms of the scale of the borders, it's mainly about the close-up vision – that is, looking at the plants at about a 45-degree angle from the adjoining path or lawn. That is not to say a New Perennials-inflected border will not work at a distance; it's just that it's not always its main interest, whereas a good colour-themed border can be enjoyed and understood in one sweeping glance.

Perhaps the most pleasing aspect of the naturalistic turn in British border design is the way the look has not become standardized, but is being evolved in different ways by different designers. With a very few exceptions, all the top names have been affected in some way, taking from it those elements which might key into their own style.

One example of this is James Alexander-Sinclair, who has redesigned the long double border at Cottesbrooke Manor, in Northamptonshire (always a garden worth watching). Experiencing it over high summer this year, it brought to mind a three-word summation of what is going on in our borders: Immersive Not Pictorial. The overwhelming impression is of being smothered (enjoyably) by a wave of verdant greenery which varies (but does not develop) along the border's length, interrupting itself with bright periods of colour from dahlias and the likes of *Cirsium heterophyllum* and *Sanguisorba officinalis* 'Arnhem'. The long view down this border is inviting, therefore, but not particularly engaging, hoticulturally. The point is, we are *in* this border, and involved in it – no longer mere observers in an outdoor picture gallery.

From the beginning there have been plenty of deniers out there, and many private gardeners understandably see no reason why they should alter garden tastes which have served us so well. But as yet there has been no co-ordinated design riposte to this stylistic change. Time for a backlash?

Garden Design Journal

ROSEMARY VEREY
NOVEMBER 2010
↔

IT IS NOW ALMOST A DECADE since the death of Rosemary Verey, gardener-owner of Barnsley House, Gloucestershire. Verey was one of the most influential designers and authors of the 1980s and 1990s, admired for elegant plantings which seemed to raise her work well above the level of the mid-century 'amiable cottage muddle' and into the realm of classic garden design. An evening held earlier this month at the Garden Museum was intended to be a timely reappraisal of her work, although it was to prove most remarkable for the biographical revelations provided by Sir Roy Strong.

But first, why the need for a reappraisal at all?

It has been the fashion in recent years to deride or ignore the Verey style. For some, she was ultimate establishment designer, a shires lady in pearls and quilted jacket who worked for the Prince of Wales at Highgrove while also enjoying a lucrative career selling her Englishness to America through books, lecture tours and garden commissions. Verey's brand of 'old-fashioned' English planting has consequently provided a convenient scapegoat for those in thrall to the new.

Her star began to wane in the early 1990s as garden style moved on from the familiar good-taste pastel tones inherited (or so it was believed) from the Arts and Crafts movement of Gertrude Jekyll, and towards the vibrant, iconoclastically exotic palette of Christopher Lloyd of Great Dixter and Nori and Sandra Pope of Hadspen. This was a long way from the Verey look, which depended on the soft tones of flowers such as alliums, 'English' (cranesbill) geraniums, campanulas, clematis and aquilegia. Also ranged in implicit opposition to the Verey approach later in the 1990s were the Modernists (led by Dan Pearson and Christopher Bradley-Hole) and, a few years on, the many who were influenced by the New Perennials approach of Dutchman Piet Oudolf and other European plantsmen.

These were matters of taste in planting, but one of the elements of Verey's style which genuinely dated quickly was the high degree of 'historical' effect in her gardens, in the form of decorative potagers, knot gardens in yew and box and small classical garden buildings (such as the eighteenth-century temple her husband, David, had installed at Barnsley House in the 1970s). Indeed, Verey's *Classic Garden Design* (1984) was subtitled 'How to Adapt and Recreate Garden Features of the Past', while her own journey towards serious gardening in late middle age was via antiquarian gardening books and manuals. But by the 1990s knot gardens, sundials and statuary seemed to many to be '*so* last decade' in style – very *Country Diary of an Edwardian Lady*, very *Brideshead*.

The Garden Museum evening, which I had the pleasure of chairing, had as its keynote speaker Barbara Paul Robinson, an American lawyer who in the 1990s spent a month working in the garden at Barnsley House and is now writing a biography of Verey. The second speaker was garden photographer Andrew Lawson, whose images – especially of the laburnum arch at Barnsley, with purple alliums below it – did a great deal to establish the Verey 'brand' in the minds of the gardening public.

But if there was any danger of the event becoming over-reverential, that was soon blown out of the water by Sir Roy Strong's contribution. He began by stressing the influence his friend had had on his own garden-making and also mentioned her 'bluestocking' credentials: despite her twinset-and-pearls appearance, Verey had studied maths and economics at London University, when she had also enjoyed japes such as waterskiing down the Thames. Sir Roy wondered, nevertheless, what had made her suddenly become completely absorbed in matters of design. Was it really old garden books, as she claimed?

Sir Roy went on to produce a startling revelation: that Verey had had a serious love affair with an interior designer who, he suggested, may have had a strong influence on her emerging design style and the layout of the garden at Barnsley in the 1970s. The identity of this designer was David Vicary, an architect whose best-known foray into garden design was the fountain garden at Wilton House. Details of the affair are recorded in a shoebox of love letters which document their trysts (now in the possession of garden designers Julian and Isabel Bannerman, who were friends of Vicary's and inherited his effects). Vicary lived at Kilvert's Parsonage, near Chippenham in Wiltshire, where his collection of furniture and *objets d'art* was admired by the cognoscenti (it is commemorated, in a sense, in a textile print by Robert Kime called 'Kilvert's Blue', based on a chintz found in the attic of the house). Vicary was a part of the wider

David Hicks circle of country house designers, though he ended up losing his mind: Sir Roy painted a vivid portrait of Vicary's tragic final days, sleeping in his car under newspapers.

The affair, according to Sir Roy, would not come as a surprise to anyone who knew Verey well. She was 'hot stuff in Gloucestershire . . . highly sexed, like many who follow the hunt' and 'the only woman I have ever known who kissed me full on the lips the very first time we met'. She was so well known for her transgressive behaviour that she was 'barred from several houses' in the county.

This was all delivered in Sir Roy's (genuinely) inimitable style. He was not at all censorious about it, noting that Verey herself had said that her marriage to David Verey had begun as a loveless one. Sir Roy believes that it continued as a marriage for appearance's sake. What raised it above the level of tittle-tattle was Sir Roy's contention that it was possibly Vicary who opened Verey's eyes to the possibilities of design, especially in a historical milieu.

The explosive nature of these revelations was made more piquant by the fact that there were about twenty Verey family members present, including three of her four children on the front row, along with the Dowager Marchioness of Salisbury. I am not sure if 'a gasp of an audience' can function as a collective noun, but that is how it felt (though I later heard that it had not come as such a surprise to several family members). As chairman, all I could do was make a weak joke about it nearly being Guy Fawkes night and thus the correct time for incendiaries.

By 'outing' Verey in this way, I do think Sir Roy was making a serious historical point, a decade after the subject's death. Such relationships are important in designers' lives, and it's a measure of Verey's legacy that it should be deemed interesting at all. What scandalized many – much more than the revelation of the affair(s) – was the implication that Verey, as a woman, would have needed this male designer to provide her with her ideas, or at least start her off on the right track. But again, I don't think Sir Roy was being misogynistic; it was just his take on this particular relationship.

As the audience emerged into a London blighted by a Tube strike, the sirens, alarms and general chaos seemed an appropriate epilogue to an event which had seen the genteel world of Cotswolds garden design turned upside down and shaken all about.

Daily Telegraph

LOST HEROES OF GARDENING

DECEMBER 2010

THE TERM 'PLANTSMAN' is used quite sparingly among experienced gardeners. (Like 'chairman', it can be used to describe both men and women – the ungainly 'plantswoman' is sometimes heard, while 'plantsperson' sounds like some sort of alien.) The 'p' word is not often invoked in vain, because gardeners at all levels are well aware of the astonishing range and complexity of the plant life available to us in Britain for cultivation – just look at the compendious *RHS Plant Finder*. For anyone to be able to grow, identify and retain a large number of unusual, rare or choice specimens is quite a feat. It's generally a lifetime's obsession, in fact, though the very best plantsmen are for ever telling you how little they know, how bad they are at gardening and so on.

This modesty (quite often false modesty, in truth), coupled with the fact that gardens of herbaceous perennials tend to disappear when their owners have snipped their last cutting, has meant that the achievements and influence of many plantsmen tend to be forgotten over time – unless they have published books, of course, which is the surest way of leaving some kind of legacy in gardening (although those books often gather dust, too). Academic garden history has tended to ignore plantsmen because of a lack of documentation and architectural interest, coupled with the amateur status of the gardeners themselves. In their time, however, and certainly in the days before television began to exert a strong influence, private individuals had a strong impact on the tastes of several generations of serious garden-makers.

So who are these lost garden heroes and heroines? A few names spring to mind immediately. John Treasure of Burford House in Shropshire was a name to conjure with in the 1960s and 1970s, especially when it came to using plants 'architecturally'. John Codrington was a designer who pushed the wild look to its limit in his own garden of intimate spaces at Stone Cottage, Northumberland, where stone paths and formal features were almost smothered with plants – rarities intermixed with quite ordinary things in an artful jumble, chosen for foliage and form as much as flower. Peter Healing at the Priory, Kemerton, Worcestershire, created effervescent planting schemes of great complexity and originality, while David Scott and Valerie Finnis at Boughton House, Northamptonshire, were famed for their expertise with alpines and just about everything else. Lionel Fortescue at The Garden House, Buckland Monachorum, Devon, was also widely admired, as was his successor at that garden, Keith Wiley, who now runs an influential nursery in Devon and ranks among those we might today call a plantsman of the old school. The current RHS president, Elizabeth Banks, and her husband, Lawrence Banks, at Hergest Croft, Worcestershire, can also be seen as a continuation of this tradition of private plantsmanship. None of these gardeners are plantsmen of the 'trainspotter' mentality – happy to grow the plants successfully and leave it at that. Their gardens are also carefully structured and aesthetically balanced, with well stocked borders complemented by woodland gardens, lawns, enclosed spaces, formal pools and garden pavilions.

The plantsman tradition dates back to the late nineteenth century and really got into its stride in the Edwardian era. The technocrat Gertrude Jekyll and her glamorous contemporary Norah Lindsay were essentially professionals, discreetly paid for their advice, but their contemporaries such as the breathless author Eleanor Vere Boyle, Avray Tipping (of *Country Life* magazine), the horti-connoisseurs E. A. Bowles and Jason Hill, Mark Fenwick of Abbotswood (a Lutyens/Jekyll garden) and the well-travelled Du Cane sisters (Ella and Florence, who made Japanese-inflected gardens in Essex) all gardened privately at a high level. Bobbie James of St Nicholas in Yorkshire was among the most respected of all, known for his massed plantings, often of single species, in enclosures. In terms of amateur plantsmanship, however, Lawrence Johnston of Hidcote – with his unlimited budget and international contacts – set the standard others aspired to. Networks of friendships extended their tentacles across the country and the tradition of gardeners visiting each other was established, with guests inevitably departing with horticultural gifts poking out of the windows and boots of their motor cars (which is exactly what happens today).

It has to be said that there was a certain relaxed air to many of the gardens made by private plantsmen as opposed to professional designers, a distinction which remains true today. It's an attitude perhaps best summed up by that doyen of the Edwardian era Canon Ellacombe, who wrote in *In My Vicarage Garden* (1902): 'Every border must be full; and for this purpose no border is given up to any one class of plants; there is a mixture of shrubs, herbaceous plants, bulbs, and ferns all joined together, without any respect to uniformity of outline, or fancied harmonies in colour, or studied variations in heights, but each placed where it grows, because that particular place was supposed to be best suited to its wants, or sometimes for no better reason than to fill a vacancy.' This approach will surely still chime with that of many gardeners today.

All these names, most of them forgotten, but many as celebrated in their day as Christopher Lloyd and Beth Chatto in our own. The great tradition continues, of course, though the opportunities in garden journalism have meant that many of those who would previously have been amateurs – gardening in the evenings, when they returned home from the bank, perhaps – are now professionally involved in horticulture, often as garden writers. Stephen Lacey, Marilyn Abbott,

Robin Lane Fox, Carol Klein, Noel Kingsbury and Tony Venison are just a few among the current generation of plantsmen.

Gardening is Britain's great vernacular art form (as the French have cooking, we have gardening) so perhaps it is fitting that our gurus should be private individuals. The only problem is, we tend to forget about them when they are gone.

Daily Telegraph

CYCLING TO GARDENS
JANUARY 2011
<>

IN THE PAST FEW YEARS I have fundamentally altered the way I approach gardens. Not the way I approach them mentally (who can legislate for that?), but the way I approach them physically. Wherever possible I will walk or – more often than not – bicycle to a garden, catching a train to the nearest station and then cycling from there. It allows one to gain an understanding of the topography which surrounds the place, something of the atmosphere of the villages and towns nearby, and also a surer feel for the physical size of the garden. If it's a large estate, with buildings or eyecatchers dotted around, you can see all sorts of things cycling the perimeter on a bike which you would miss in a car – most dramatically at Hagley in Worcestershire, where the eighteenth-century landscape park is bisected by a dual carriageway, with temples and obelisks appearing on both sides in rapid succession. Some gardens even have bicycle racks (nearly always empty).

You do get some rather strange looks, arriving on a bike, but it's quite nice to be eccentric sometimes. I shall never forget the look of amazement on Isabel Bannerman's face as I cycled straight into the gatehouse at Hanham Court, her home near Bath. Cycling up from the station at Keynsham I had gained a keen sense of the steepness of the hills around there and of the meandering course of the river

Avon. The nature of local woodland and even what is growing well in local gardens can be of relevance to the garden enthusiast, easily missed in a car.

It's partly the speed of motoring today. If one reads garden writing of the early to mid twentieth century there tends to be much more of a sense of place and topography. In Christopher Hussey's multi-part articles on country houses in *Country Life* magazine, for example, the first instalment was always about the local topography and landscape. One imagines him driving the lanes at a stately pace – or, more likely, being driven – in an open-topped motor car. Gertrude Jekyll and Edwin Lutyens got around the byways of Surrey – so influential for both of them – in a little gig, laughing and sketching as they went, rather than speeding through villages. How else could Jekyll have sketched all those gates and fences for her book on West Surrey?

This bicycling agenda is not, I hasten to add, some sort of one-man ecological crusade, or the result of my driving licence being confiscated. It has arisen because I am not a natural motorist and tend to arrive in a somewhat frazzled state if I have driven any distance. It can take a while for the mind to cool down after a long journey, to recover from the stress of traffic jams, unscheduled roadworks and aggressive drivers, and it seems a shame to go through a garden in a dizzied daze having travelled all that way.

This is all sounding very virtuous, isn't it? Well, there are other benefits to eschewing the car. One shouldn't cycle around drunk, of course, but going by bike does mean you can enjoy a glass or two of wine with lunch in the garden restaurant if you are going with pals. And surely the exercise will balance out the effects of that treacle pudding and cream ...

Perhaps the best way of understanding the topography of a garden is by staying there. Not many of us are on the weekend guest list of places like Chatsworth, but it is certainly possible to rent estate buildings and apartments at numerous fine gardens looked after by the National Trust and Landmark Trust – the Gothic Temple at Stowe, for example, or the famous Pineapple folly at Dunmore, in Scotland. This way, you can experience the garden over a longer period and in all moods – the moods of both you and the garden, that is, for a garden visit is essentially a dialogue.

For an even more intimate exposure to a garden's topography, what about camping in it? There are not many opportunities for this, but one I found particularly rewarding was at Port Eliot in Cornwall, a fine Repton-influenced estate on the banks of the Tamar which runs its own summer festival each year. You can pitch your tent more or less where you like, and I enjoyed emerging bleary-eyed to contemplate the mighty oaks of the park. Sleeping on the ground is guaranteed to instil a sense of place in the camper.

Daily Telegraph

SUPER-SHACKS
JULY 2011
⤝

VISITORS to the summer garden shows often complain of the 'unreality' of the show gardens – or so we are told by sections of the media, though I have never heard a 'real' person air such views. I seem to spend a lot of time defending the likes of the Chelsea show each year, and it strikes me that one area where sceptical comments might be justifiable is with regard to the structures in these gardens: all those shelters, pavilions, huts, sheds, home offices, guest suites, pool houses, writing dens, outdoor kitchens and havens of meditation. As a typology, these *fabriques* constitute a highly refined genre of architecture which is only really seen at shows such as Chelsea and Hampton Court: the 'super-shack'.

Super-shacks often take up a lot of room on a show garden site and I don't really understand why. Yes, in some instances the whole *raison d'être* of the garden is bound up with its sponsorship by the manufacturers of some hideous eco-friendly home office, replete with solar panels, green roof, water recycling technology and comfy beanbags (why all the beanbags?). But in many cases the super-shack is there for no good reason, in terms of design. It just gets in the way, or else seems superfluous, lurking at the back of the garden with its furniture, trying so hard to be modish, and so often failing.

In a garden of the size of a typical Chelsea plot, it would be unthinkable to erect a large stucture, and certainly no competent designer would suggest it. The conservatory attached to the house or, in less suburban mode, the extended glass-walled kitchen, is a much more likely option. In show gardens the super-shack is generally found towards the rear of the garden – creating what is known as the 'shack at the back' syndrome – and can easily dominate the look of the whole space, since it often takes up the entire width of the garden and is the largest 'thing' in it by some distance. More often than not, it brings the whole design down a notch or two. This was certainly the case across the board at Chelsea this year, with the exception of James Wong's garden, where the pavilion was one of the elements which moulded space in a meaningful way.

What are these super-shacks for? Surely clients don't really need a bespoke structure just in order to shelter from the rain – there are plenty of other places to do that. It seems to me that these strange little edifices function as pseudo-houses, intended to create a sense that the design has some relevance to the real world because it contains a sheltered place where a person can sit down in peace. The super-shack can also create a useful variation in scale, the uniformity of its facade offsetting the complexity of the planting, as demanded by the flower show's rules. But all too often the super-shack has a lumpen presence, completely at odds with anything you are likely to see in the real world, since pavilions or shelters need careful siting in lots of space and rarely form the focus for a garden. The best show gardens, like Cleve West's winning offering at Chelsea this year, manage to do without super-shacks altogether.

Indeed, have you ever seen one of these things in a real garden? They are extremely rare. The one at Bury Court in Hampshire, by Christopher Bradley-Hole, springs to mind, but one has the sense that it was built chiefly in order to be photographed. Real garden pavilions are often quite ramshackle, leftover versions of something else.

I was recently put on the spot about Chelsea and the other flower shows by a visitor from abroad who argued, given that planting design is at such a premium at the shows, that it might be better simply to give each entrant a rectangular plot and invite them to fill it with plants. This sounded like a counsel of despair to me, but on the other hand I can think of only two mainstream (that is, non-conceptual) show gardens that have struck me as really well designed.

The first was Christopher Bradley-Hole's now near-legendary 1997 Chelsea garden, which successfully united Modernist design with naturalistic planting. The second was Tom Stuart-Smith's 2006 garden, with rusted Corten steel water-tanks, multi-stemmed *Viburnum rhytidophyllum* and masses of box and hornbeam. What these two gardens had in common – together with a sure handling of space and structure and a deft arrangement of tone and texture – was that the existence of a shelter or resting place was only implied, its elements firmly a part of the continuum of the design, not an interruption of it.

Not so long ago, cars were allowed on show gardens at Chelsea and Hampton Court. Perhaps now it's time for us to wave goodbye to the super-shack, as well.

Garden Design Journal

NATURAL PLAYSPACE
SEPTEMBER 2011

↬

'STOP THE CAR!' yelled my two boys in unison as we drove past the local park near our home in what is sometimes described as a 'leafy suburb' of north London. Wondering what terrifying emergency situation might be unfolding around us, I pulled over, only to find that they had already leapt out and were running excitedly into the park. When I caught up with them, it transpired that the reason for the urgency was a large, new castle-like edifice, lying on its side in the fenced-off section of the park, awaiting placement as part of a hotly anticipated, newly designed playspace. 'Wow!' they exclaimed, imagining their ascent of this structure when the railings come down (and clearly trying to figure out a way of achieving this goal before that moment). As is the case with most small boys, one of their main interests in life is climbing things – the higher the better.

The 'castle' edifice is literally the high point of a new timber-built playground area which will replace a variety of other structures deemed to be unsafe or old-fashioned. The project has caused a certain amount of dissent and division among local parents, since people can become rather attached to playground equipment over the years, but the children now seem to be relishing the prospect of something new. (It can be difficult to gauge what children want, anyway: I recently attended a one-day conference on 'the future of play' where one 'playworker' told me that when you ask children what they would like to see in a new playground, they invariably suggest one of three things: a swimming pool, a roller coaster, or an ice-cream van. Another common request is perhaps more achievable: drinking-water fountains.)

What is noticeable about our new local playspace – and many others which have been taking shape in parks around the country in the past couple of years – is that it is a 'natural' playground. That is, the equipment is made of rough recycled logs and the general aesthetic is of a woodland glade where children can frolic amid nature in a thoroughly wholesome way. The swings and roundabouts of yore are being sidelined in favour of wood-and-rope climbing structures or play areas made of rocks, pieces of timber and sand which in many cases look like natural features. The new mantra is that an old tree trunk on its side, with its roots in the air, is more fun for children than a slide on an island of asphalt. There are a lot of new playspaces about – many of them 'natural' – because some £350 million of government money has been poured into the Play Builder scheme in recent years. (Predictably, the money has now dried up.)

Playground design makes a difference to the majority of local park users – not just the minority who are/have young children – because it has a dramatic impact on the overall look of the place, especially if the acreage is not large. Perhaps it's good news that the old, fenced-off and segregated areas of incongruously brightly coloured play equipment are gradually being replaced in this way, because natural playspaces are certainly more attractive.

From a gardening point of view, the natural playground offers more scope for horticultural creativity. Mature trees are at a premium, there is grass all around instead of asphalt, and there are even play features made of plants – such as mazes made of grasses and woven-willow play dens and other structures – and insect-friendly plantations to encourage the 'mini-beasts', as children call them nowadays.

There are designers in Scandinavia and Germany who offer a relatively 'pure' take on the natural playground idea – people like Helle Nebelong in Copenhagen, who likes to use only materials found on site in the creation of play areas, envisaging an unbounded playspace which becomes a part of the whole park, as opposed to being a segregated section. A typical Nebelong play area consists of logs, tree trunks, rocks, stone and sand, ranged around a large, undulating area of trees and long grass which may contain artificially landformed mounds. I don't know of any such examples in this country, as yet – most natural playspaces in Britain remain just as dependent on 'equipment' as traditional examples, and a cynic could argue that the towers, climbing frames and slides in the catalogues of the (mostly German-based) manufacturers are simply natural-wood versions of what we had before.

A natural playground can nevertheless be a hard sell initially to children and parents suspicious of change. But when they get to play on them, children do seem to love the sense of risk and challenge offered by these structures. One of my boys managed to get a rope-burn on his eyelid, of all places, on the natural play structure now in Regent's Park (near the zoo), but he was having so much fun, he didn't mind – and so neither did I.

Daily Telegraph, Medlar column

FIFTH SEASON
SEPTEMBER 2011

✧

PERHAPS NOW IS THE TIME to acknowledge that a 'fifth season' has emerged in gardening – the period we are enjoying now, late summer merging into early autumn. In the minds of most gardeners, surely this time of year offers something quite distinct from the delights of summer and autumn?

It's certainly the case that late summer has become the most fashionable moment of the gardening calendar – just look at all the attention now lavished on those plants which look their best as the evenings become shorter, sharper and chillier. Grasses waving gently in the breeze and capturing the general russet-brown feel of the season; tall perennials whose flowering may be 'over' but which are very far from over in terms of structure; 'prairie' daisy flowers adding an incongruous note of bright yellow or orange. It's almost as if the gardening style of the moment – a kind of composed naturalism – has ensured that this is the time of the year when our plantings appear to be most up to date, chic and sophisticated (in theory, at least). To think that just a few years ago, late summer in British gardens was in many cases geared to displays of asters and dahlias, planted out almost as single-species displays.

The reasons for the emergence of the 'fifth season' in gardening are chiefly bound up with the generally more naturalistic current of planting style which has developed in this country in the past few decades. It began as a more relaxed, let-it-all-hang-out attitude in the early 1990s, with plant choice affected by Beth Chatto's gravel garden in Essex. It was then decisively influenced by Piet Oudolf and the New Perennials movement from the Netherlands and Germany. Now, the extreme naturalism of the Sheffield School and the legacy of planting gurus such as the late Henk Gerritsen are beginning to take effect, a theory of horticulture which is inexorably geared to the final flush of summer.

The result has been that the British planting palette is no longer based on the colour theory of Jekyll and the Arts and Crafts movement; indeed, it's no longer a 'palette' at all, since colour is deemed of secondary importance to form. And the 'tapestry' effect of the cottage garden, as promoted mid twentieth century by Vita Sackville-West, Margery Fish and many others, has been superseded by a concentration on plantings which function as a continuum, chiefly as a result of the different rhythms produced by repeat plantings. Those rhythms can be created in different ways, either as drift plantings which repeat down a perspective view, or as rivulets of colour and shape which cut through other massed plantings, or as bright markers which add highlights at carefully judged intervals (sedums at the fronts of beds are an example of this). The Jekyllian garden is often associated with the visual impact of Impressionist painting, whereas today's emphasis on rhythm would perhaps call for a musical analogy instead – that's certainly the way Tom Stuart-Smith looks at it.

This kind of planting comes into its own in late summer, when large drifts, banks and rivulets of perennials, framed by grasses and shrubs, really start to express their personality. It would be tempting to observe that the likes of miscanthus, stipa, molinia and pennisetum are the mainstay of the late-summer garden – and judging by the focus of many of the books available on the topic, one would say that. But grasses are arguably not as noticeable in gardens as they were, say, five years ago, and tend to be used with more care and discernment. The fear among some plantsmen was that grasses would completely displace shrubs, but that has not happened.

There are other, more down-to-earth reasons for the emergence of the fifth season. Climate change has, we are told, led to longer, milder summers and delayed the onset of autumn, and gardeners' ecological concerns have found an outlet in a planting style which in theory demands less maintenance and in many cases no watering. The expansive nature of many of the perennials used has meant there is less call for annuals and other 'fillers' in the late-summer border. A wilder look also appears to attract more wildlife – though that may be illusory. And of course the nursery trade has been enthusiastically promoting the deployment of a new generation of grasses and perennials – or rather, old plants used in new ways.

But what do we call this new fifth gardening season? Perhaps we ought to label it simply 'late summer' as opposed to 'early autumn', since those rich flower hues, decorously decaying stems and seedheads, and the palpably elegiac quality of the light all conspire to give these weeks the feel of a 'late' period. To use an art-historical analogy, late summer is the rococo period to the baroque of high summer, to the renaissance of spring. (I'm not sure what mannerism in the garden would be – answers on a postcard?)

Country Life

GAY GARDENING
OCTOBER 2011

THE RECENT PUBLICATION of a book called *Sister Arts: The Erotics of Lesbian Landscapes* by Lisa L. Moore gives rise to reflections on the subject of gay gardening. Does sexual orientation have any relevance in the world of garden design? Having been something of a taboo subject until relatively recently, the academic discipline of 'queer theory' is now making inroads into gardening – see also *Queer Ecologies: Sex, Nature, Politics, Desire* (2010).

It now seems to be acceptable in conversation to speculate, for example, as to whether Lawrence Johnston of Hidcote was gay – Sir Roy Strong posed the question directly on a television documentary recently, noting that Johnston may have turned to gardening partly to get away from his domineering mother, and speculating as to whether he ever made his way down to the docks for a spot of hanky panky with a sailor. Crikey! Whatever happened to the (sexless) Edwardian gardens of a golden afternoon which we all celebrated in the 1980s? Whatever next? 'The Country Sex Diary of an Edwardian Lady'? On a more serious note, it was salutary that the winner of last year's conceptual section at Hampton Court was the 'Pansy Project' garden, which commemorated people injured or killed in homophobic street attacks.

Yes, the stereotypes are painful and even having this discussion will make many a gay person wince at the vulgarity, prurience and impertinence of it all, but surely everyone in the gardens world knows that gay men often make excellent horticulturists and garden designers. So many great gardens of the past have been made by men described as 'lifelong bachelors' who 'never married' (as if they just forgot to). It is almost as if the gardening gene has somehow been harnessed to the gay gene? (As if . . .)

Making reference to this has historically been taboo, until 1967 partly for legal reasons and more recently because it is simply impolite to speculate about someone's sexuality unless they introduce the topic themselves. In his lifetime no one ever published the suggestion that Christo Lloyd, for example, was homosexual, though it is assumed 'everyone knew' (I have my doubts about that). Lloyd's friend Derek Jarman was 'out', on the other hand, and very publicly dying from Aids (to use the parlance of the time). The fact that Jarman was out and active makes me consider his garden in the context of 1980s gender politics and the Aids phenomenon, whereas all of that seems far less relevant to the world of Great Dixter. Now that so many gay gardeners are contentedly 'out' (true of the men, at least) – and I've noticed increased relaxation about this even over the past five years – it's likely that this is a topic which will be grappled with at a more serious level.

Everything has been more difficult for gay women, needless to say. Societal constraints meant that gardening of any kind was deemed 'unladylike' up until the Edwardian period, though on the other hand close intimacy between women was far more normalized in polite society than it was for men. *Lesbian Landscapes* views the eighteenth-century world of female picturesque garden making and grotto decoration in this milieu as an expression of that intimacy and sorority – though in the process it does seek to 'out' certain women as lesbians on little or no actual evidence (as tends to be the way with queer theory).

It is tempting to speculate about what it is that draws gay men and women to gardening. The importance of friendship, for one, and in earlier times gardening's convenience as a social conduit. The garden is traditionally a place of solace and escape, where gender differences are blurred or compromised: in the garden, women can do more 'manly' things, like physical labour, while men can engage in more 'feminine' pursuits, such as designing borders. For men, too, one of the attractions of solo physical work is that it is a means of physical expression which is worlds away from the tyranny of organized sport and its traditions of homophobia.

Then there is the satisfaction of design itself, which for some reason tends to be held in higher regard by many gay people. One is on shakier ground with any suggestion that garden making might become some kind of substitute for having a family or children, an idea you sometimes hear ventured. It's true that gardening satisfies a deep urge to nurture, but I'm not at all sure whether that is akin to nurturing human beings.

So, to summarize (and I'm not even going to get into bisexuality): being gay does not make you good at gardening, and not all good gardeners are gay. It's just that it appears, anecdotally, that you are more likely to be good at gardening if you are gay. Is that fair?

Garden Design Journal

THE CHELSEA FRINGE
JANUARY 2012
⊕

MOST READERS will by now be aware – I hope! – of the inaugural Chelsea Fringe festival, which is happening over three weeks, from 19 May to 10 June 2012. The intention with this initiative (which I dreamt up one day during Chelsea 2010) was to tap into the excitement around the time of Chelsea Flower Show and thereby to encourage all sorts of people to get involved with garden events. The aim was to burst out of the Chelsea showground in every way – demographically, to reach all those who would not think of visiting the main show; conceptually, to widen out our idea of what gardens and gardening can be; and geographically, in that the Fringe events are happening across London, not just in the vicinity of affluent Chelsea. In time – say, five to ten years – I believe this could be a national event, and indeed there are events being organized outside London in this first year.

Having had the idea, I found I had to fight to keep the Fringe both independent of the RHS and non-commercial in essence, and I soon found myself working in a voluntary capacity as its founding director. As you can imagine, this has been challenging but also extremely rewarding, as it has put me in contact with all kinds of interesting and inspiring people who operate on the fringes of the garden world (which is fitting for a Fringe, of course). As this column goes to press, the Fringe is still unsponsored and is being co-ordinated by a small but dedicated band of volunteers, many of them garden designers and members of the Society of Garden Designers. Annabel Downs, chair of the SGD, is on the Fringe steering committee alongside designers including Cleve West. Many of those creating events for the Fringe are garden or landscape designers, or else interior designers with an interest in exteriors, too.

I didn't want anything in the Fringe to overlap with what visitors might get to see at a Royal Horticultural Society show, not just to avoid treading on the RHS's toes but more importantly to provide a genuinely alternative offer – edgy, surprising, fun, and at times positively 'lo-fi' as opposed to high-budget. In this spirit, garden designers are not designing 'show gardens' for the Fringe. They are 'guerilla gardening', and co-ordinating community vegetable growing; they are creating fantasy installations in unlikely places; they are making imaginative public spaces (which will remain permanent) in difficult areas of the city; they are curating walks and talks (foraging in Hackney!); they are co-ordinating direct interactions with the public at street level (plant giveways and spontaneous workshops); they are making gardens which are portable, modular or transportable.

It seems to me that the kind of activities being dreamt up by garden designers for the Fringe could also be the kind of things which the profession might do more of in the 'real world' – not that the Fringe is unreal, in that the idea is that as many projects as possible will continue to have a life far beyond the three weeks of the festival, to get away from the unsustainable garden show model. Community interaction in urban areas seems to be a particularly fruitful area of engagement. The success of so many small-scale community garden projects implies that people in towns and cities across Britain are desperate for a greener environment over which they can exert control, a place where fruit and veg can be grown, where flowers can cheer, and where they can get to know like-minded neighbours while improving the environment for everyone.

Generally such ventures are started by local people and sometimes fostered by specialized charities such as Capital Growth or Green Corners; there are now grants galore for this kind of activity. Perhaps qualified garden designers can start playing a bigger role, helping to lead the regeneration of our towns and cities from the ground up, from the most 'local' basis imaginable, as opposed to pandering to local authorities' reliance on lofty systematic plans dreamt up by the new cadre of landscape urbanists emerging from within the landscape profession.

The Chelsea Fringe is a good place to start the process – and it's certainly not too late to get involved, either as a volunteer or as the instigator of a project or event.

Garden Design Journal

TREE PLANTING

JANUARY 2012

A SUDDEN AND IRRESISTIBLE URGE to plant trees is a syndrome which seems to hit many a plutocratic male with acres as he enters his sixties. This appears to be a deep-seated, almost primal urge. It can manifest itself as an arboretum of rarities dotted around what had been a little-used paddock; avenues at every entrance so that guests are left in no doubt that they are entering a real demesne; or perhaps a deciduous woodland planted, with a dramatically altruistic flourish, for the benefit of generations to come.

But tree planting need not be considered a selfless act – nor, indeed, as the sole preserve of men of a certain age. To begin with, the rewards of trees are far more immediate than is commonly supposed. It is nearly always assumed that the selfless planter of trees will not live long enough to be able to enjoy his or her young charges in their full majesty. That may be true in the case of oaks and other forest trees, if all one craves is an ancient tree of massive aspect and gnarled complexion, but a lot of pleasure can be derived from trees which are between five and twenty-five years old. Trees grow and change remarkably rapidly, year on year, as their natural characteristics come into their own, and the planter can see significant changes in a landscape even over a period of five to ten years.

It is by no means absurd, therefore, for a septuagenarian or even an octogenarian to start a tree-planting campaign. Indeed, as Alan Mitchell, universally acknowledged as the greatest British tree expert of the twentieth century, once pointed out, there is more pleasure to be had from a young tree of up to ten years old than from a mature specimen, because the youngster not only changes dramatically every year, but can be observed in detail at close quarters, on a more human scale, as it pops into leaf or establishes its distinctive shape. Ancient trees, on the other hand, basically remain the same to human eyes once they reach full maturity. If a young person in arboricultural terms – that is to say, someone in reasonable health before their sixtieth year – starts thinking about planting trees, they can expect to see something substantial well within their lifetime. And that time will surely fly by – as the National Trust's first gardens adviser, Graham Stuart Thomas, once observed, of a landscape shaped by trees: 'Fifty years is a long time in anticipation, but short in retrospect.'

Tree planting is not necessarily about collecting different varieties, either: there is a great deal of aesthetic and creative gratification to be had from working with common native trees, specifically thinking about their placement. In fact, this is the aspect of tree husbandry which the most experienced arborists value above all. As Hugh Johnson, the noted tree (and wine) expert observes: 'The spaces between the trees are even more important than the trees themselves – you've got to think of the context.'

Kim Wilkie, a landscape architect well used to working on large private estates, concurs with this view: 'It's all about framing and designing with blocks of woodland to accentuate the character of the estate. I planted ten acres of new woodland nearly twenty years ago and it looks fine now.' Wilkie also emphasizes the financial and ecological potential of planting native deciduous woodland or coppiced woodland: 'It's the best kind of habitat you can get for wildlife,' he says. 'It's often very good for shooting purposes. And one of the most dramatic changes to estate management of the past few years has been using woodland as a renewable source of woodchip, which has now become a viable alternative to oil. More and more people are heating the main house, the cottages and the glasshouses using woodchip. Ash and sweet chestnut are among the best species to use. Ash is the wonder tree of Britain at the moment – sometimes it's called a weed tree but it's my favourite. If you look at Gainsborough's paintings, he uses it all the time.'

So, what to plant, and where? Soil and climatic conditions are obviously of vital importance, but before one starts to worry about practical issues the most important thing is to decide upon an aesthetic objective. Most private individuals plant trees because they want to improve the look of their estate or large garden, and some thought needs to be given to the kind of atmosphere one is looking to create. If it's a naturalistic, picturesque, traditionally English look, then it will be a matter of planting classic trees such as common oak, beech or sycamore, with nothing fancy in terms of colour, form or variegated leaf. Maples which go bright red in autumn, copper beeches, or fastigiate or weeping forms should be eschewed entirely.

That is certainly the advice from Hugh Johnson: 'I would say: shun the red tree or the golden tree. Avoid the extraordinary. They are not necessary. It's easy to forget that a copper beech just creates a great black hole in the garden all summer long. People are welcome to magnolias but if you have a tree that's an event once a year, it's not an event the rest of the year. I have fifty-foot oaks I planted myself.'

The advice is that one should try to look at key vistas critically. Is the scene too clear and therefore bland in the foreground? The foreground might benefit from being broken up with clumps, or trees which can lead the eye on into the distant landscape. Any drama, in terms of contour or water, should be accentuated. Are the lines of fences or walls too definite – might they be taken out or softened by the addition of trees, or be re-sited so they at least follow the contours of the land? In many cases the more distant views might be blocked out by stands of trees which could be removed or thinned, or there might be anomalous tree species in sight – a lone scrawny Scots pine, perhaps – which could be taken out of the picture.

The effect of shadows must be assessed, and reflections in water. Trees around rivers and lakes should not overcrowd the banks, but be used to accentuate the shape of the watercourse or pond. Light-foliaged trees might profitably be placed in the foreground, followed by the mid-greens of oaks, hornbeams, chestnuts, limes and ash, and then the dark tones of yew, pine, firs and Turkey oaks, against which lighter trees such as willows might sing out. In short, the estate owner must try to think like Humphry Repton, who created his celebrated Red Books containing 'before-and-after' images of estates and gardens.

Trees may be planted primarily for practical reasons: to screen out unwanted buildings, neighbours, pylons or roads, for example (in the last case, also acting as a noise barrier). In terms of common trees, a good rule of thumb is: hornbeam and oak on heavy soils; beech on chalk; sweet chestnut, birch and pine on sand; sycamore and ash on widswept rocky uplands; and willows and poplars for moist ground. When it comes to planting shelterbelts on high ground, it's often a good idea to restrict their composition to just two kinds of tree, perhaps with a few poplars dotted here and there to break up any uniformity of height.

If, on the other hand, what you really want is a collection of rare trees from the Himalayas, north America, southern Europe, Australia, the Brazilian rainforests and beyond, then you should prepare for a lifetime's hobby, and not one which everyone will appreciate. As with those men who choose to erect a model railway in the living room, so not everyone will understand the urge to create a forest of fifty eucalyptus species in Surrey. Having made this point, one has to admit that a really good arboretum made by a dedicated and knowledgeable owner – such as that at the Quinta in Lancashire, which belongs to the astronomer Sir Bernard Lovell – is an awe-inspiring and admirable sight.

Tree planting on a large scale can be a daunting prospect, however, in which case it can make sense to call in a professional. Michael Lear is probably the most respected tree expert working in Britain today, with a pragmatically ecumenical attitude to the arboreal tastes of his clients. 'I know a few eucalyptus arboreta in southern England and they look like New South Wales,' he says. 'I made one myself for the National Trust at Plas Newydd in the 1990s. These things fit into the horticultural spectrum.'

Lear likes to use a mix of trees which are young and old, in two age ranges: some about three years old, and some twelve to thirteen years old. 'Five or six years on, sometimes the young stuff will have grown incredibly well and look completely different,' he says. 'But we can include older stock – it depends on how much of a hurry the client is in. It's a lot more expensive to plant mature trees, partly because you are dealing with plants that are more than a ton in weight, which need transporting and planting.' A fully mature specimen tree can cost more than £1,000 – and almost as much again for planting services (though those costs go down if a number of trees are to be planted in one go). Bundles of knee-high 'whips' will cost far less (50p to £2 each), but will, of course, take longer to grow.

'A simple deciduous mix would be holly, thorn, oak, hazel and field maple,' Lear explains. 'You have different heights and longevity, and both evergreen and deciduous. That's a really good matrix and if you plant them irregularly it can look lovely after a few years, with just a bit of thinning. Sometimes you can put in smaller shrubs, like honeysuckles to grow up the oaks, and think of it in terms of layering.'

'I'm always mindful that if you just plant trees and no shrubs, you can end up looking at a lot of stems. Arboreta in particular have to be carefully handled – internal structure, such as a hedge system, can be the answer.'

In common with all English arborists, Lear loves to use oaks, including the common oak, the sessile oak and the Lucombe oak, a hybrid which he praises highly. 'They grow very vigorously and in the storms of 1987 and 1990 they proved to be one of the most wind-firm trees – hardly any of them blew over. If you want an amazing statement in the landscape (and some of them are evergreen, as well), you can't beat them.'

Hugh Johnson agrees that there is no reason to pay large sums for numerous mature trees, for a quick result – 'I would say: plant small and plant thick. It was Repton who told us that to dot a few starveling saplings on an open lawn is a recipe for ugliness and disaster. As for planting, small maidens [one-year-old whips] are absolutely ideal – nothing bigger, unless you are going for something that is absolutely mature. But there is such joy in the detail of young trees: the jewellery of new leaves, buds, twigs and so on.'

Johnny Phibbs of Debois Landscape Survey Group is a leading expert on the landscape design of 'Capability' Brown, and as such one would expect him to be a promoter of the English landscape tradition. 'I think the English tradition is about moulding and sculpting shapes using the materials that lie to hand, so that the thing we make appears not be made,' he explains. 'It entails an element of modesty, the idea that it's better to plant groups of beech as opposed to avenues of Wellingtonia. When I started I was constantly having to restrain people who wanted to buy copper beeches as opposed to common beeches.'

Phibbs's advice is also to think about maintenance at an early stage, especially the spacing of trees so that machinery and if necessary the lawnmower can get through. 'I'm very keen on planting trees in small clumps with guards on, so that livestock can do the grazing around them. With bigger plantations, it can be very pleasurable looking after the trees yourself. You can plant whips and prune early, after just a few years, by selecting a leader and pruning to that, and you don't even have to clear up all the twigs as you go. You can leave it on the ground and just call it brash.' He also recommends planting whips at about knee height – birch, ash and alder are quick-growing – intermixed with some older specimens. 'You'll have something to look at in less than ten years,' he says.

One thing that unites all leading arborists in Britain is their enthusiasm for oaks, and especially the common oak, *Quercus robur*. As Johnny Phibbs says: 'The oak is the tree most bound up with our national story, and it's lucky that the oak is best for building purposes, for species and nature conservation, and the best-looking. It's not a fast grower, but it will grow just about anywhere.'

So, it seems, the core pieces of advice from the experts can be summarized as: plant oaks, and plant plenty of them. And: you're never too old to start.

Financial Times

YELLOW BOOK
MARCH 2012
↝

THIS IS THE TIME OF YEAR when keen garden visitors start thumbing through the National Garden Scheme's *Yellow Book* of private gardens open to the public for a few days or weekends each year. Celebrating its 85th anniversary in 2012, the NGS is a national institution of which we can still be unequivocally proud. It's not only a reflection of our love of good gardens – and of good home-made cakes – but also raises millions of pounds (£2.6 million last year) for a variety of charities including Macmillan Cancer Support, Marie Curie Cancer Care and Help for Hospices. And it's all driven by goodwill and voluntarism – home-owners opening up their private domains to the prying eyes of hordes of strangers. Who says an Englishman's home is his castle?

The term 'bible' is rather over-used when it comes to guide books, but in the case of the *Yellow Book* it makes sense: this chunky tome lists some 3,800 gardens and a total of 7,727 open days. It's Genesis is Bedfordshire and its Revelations is Powys. Each entry is a brief description of what visitors can expect of the garden visit, from grand country houses with acres, to picture-postcard cottages (lots of those), to tiny back gardens in urban areas (not so many). The only thing the *Yellow Book* cannot reliably inform us about is the weather. Chairman Penny Snell refers darkly to 2011's 'Black Sunday', 12 June, one of the NGS's biggest weekends, when it poured with rain across the country. (Surely nothing a nice cup of tea can't fix, though.)

There is one eccentricity about the *Yellow Book* which I have not seen remarked upon: the fact that all the descriptive entries are written by the garden owners themselves. This lends an intriguing frisson to the guide, with the personalities of the owners coming through, as well as some unintentionally revealed subtexts.

What are we to make of the killer brackets deployed by Sprint Mill, in Cumbria, which is an 'unorthodox organic garden (atypical NGS)'? And how can anyone compete with the opening line of the entry for a garden in Ayot St Lawrence, Hertfordshire: 'Enter through adjacent romantic church ruins . . .'? There are as many 'stunning' and 'spectacular' gardens as there are 'charming' and 'peaceful', though only a daring few claim to be 'magnificent'. Town gardens are usually described as 'hidden gems', while those which have been 'designed' invariably boast that Holy Grail of NGS horticulture 'year-round colour'. The words 'artists' garden fantasy' may or may not set off alarm bells.

An element of competition creeps into the London entries, a number of which claim to be 'popular' or even 'enduringly popular'. Unusual features – the 'Seven Dwarfs' Bank'? – are designed to intrigue, but one must be careful not to over-sell things like 'fabulous large fuchsias' (they'd better be). On the other hand, only the hard-core are likely to be excited by the promise of a 'flourishing bog'. Still, on the subject of dwarfs, Berkshire's 'small urban gardeners' garden' inspires a vision of town-based gnomes merrily gardening away. And one garden is described as 'mature but enduring' (aren't we all, dear?)

There is an undercurrent of anxiety running through many *Yellow Book* entries. It's understandable – who would not be nervous about opening up the garden to paying visitors? People are no more likely to be forgiving because it's 'all for charity'. Algernon Heber-Percy of Hodnet Hall in Shropshire ('unique collection of big-game trophies in tea room') tells the story of the visitor who, hearing that the garden had been opening for the NGS for more than eighty years, was heard to mutter, 'You'd think they'd have done more with the place.'

Yellow Book gardens self-described as 'created with passion' or 'much-loved' are sounding a warning: 'Please be gentle with us', they seem to plead. The nervous energy being expended can be palpable, as with Mrs Birnhak's garden in Balham, south London, opening on 27 May only: 'Weather permitting, Anne's eponymous Floribunda rose should be flowering.' Those first two words say it all for gardeners. Good luck, Mrs Birnhak.

Daily Telegraph, Medlar column

RODMARTON
JUNE 2012
✧

ONE OF MY FAVOURITE GARDENS in the world is that of Rodmarton Manor, in Gloucestershire, an Arts and Crafts garden of outdoor rooms, topiary, high brick walls and gorgeous tapestry-style planting. When I mentioned my preference to the *Telegraph*'s garden editor she was surprised that I should be so keen on it, as she associated my tastes more with either the inscrutably avant-garde or the wonders of the eighteenth-century landscape garden. Some critics – me included – have almost vilified Arts and Crafts style for the way it dominated British garden making through the twentieth century, becoming responsible for a kind of 'good-taste' gardening which was as much about keeping up with the Joneses as anything else. So why on earth should I be waxing lyrical about this place?

A bit of self-examination was called for. After careful thought I can say that my reasoning might be summed up in one word: authenticity. It is this which keeps drawing me back to the garden.

Because Rodmarton Manor is real Arts and Crafts. Not National Trust Arts and Crafts (like Sissinghurst); not faux Arts and Crafts (like East Ruston Manor in Norfolk); not chocolate-box cottagey Arts and Crafts; not the rather snobby, shabby chic version of Arts and Crafts which still pervades British garden style. Rodmarton cannot be held responsible for the imitative and miniaturized style of Arts and Crafts which began to pervade British gardens in the interwar years, when the kitsch delights of decorative wishing wells, crazy paving, tiny formal pools and lines of rose standards began to proliferate. Rodmarton's garden was the real thing at the time and remains so today. A visit to this garden can give you an authentic savour of what Arts and Crafts meant to those disciples of William Morris who practised their crafts so assiduously and passionately in the first decades of the twentieth century. And that is an extremely delicate and valuable thing.

The people who built the house and garden at Rodmarton from scratch between 1909 and 1929 were Claud and Margaret Biddulph, a stockbroker and his wife with 'progressive' views and the money to realize their ideals. They envisaged a large village house (it was only dubbed a 'manor' later on) which would be an experiment in communitarian living, with people coming every day from the village to the house to work on serious craft projects, such as carpentry and tapestry. The garden's bones were laid out by the architect Ernest Barnsley, while Margaret Biddulph and her head gardener, William Scrubey, filled in the horticultural detail. Margaret herself was a trained horticulturist, having attended Studley Horticultural College for Women, one of several such institutions which flourished in the Edwardian period.

What is unusual about Rodmarton is that it was made in the true spirit of the Arts and Crafts movement as imagined by William Morris and his disciples. The house blends with the garden, exactly as Morris enjoined, by means of the extraordinary and unique terrace containing high hedges which stretches along the south side of the house. With just one full-time gardener, Rodmarton cannot quite compete with Sissinghurst and Hidcote as a sustained horticultural extravaganza. However, it has arguably retained more of its original spirit than either of those gardens, mainly because it remains in the hands of the family that commissioned it in the first place, and is kept up in the spirit originally envisaged.

It is the terrace with its associated gardens directly south of the house which is the really original feature at Rodmarton, in that the clipped yew hedges are not simply decorative but create coherent architectural spaces. The intense arrangement of yew interrupted by mature Portuguese laurels creates a sense that these are exterior rooms which are physically conjoined with the house. As William Morris himself wrote in 1895 (of an imaginary property): 'The garden, divided by old clipped yew hedges, is quite unaffected and very pleasant, and looks in fact as if it were a part of the house, or at least the clothes of it; which I think ought to be the aim of the layer-out of the garden.' Morris would also have approved of the rambling roses which add homely colour to the terrace in summer.

Adjacent to the terrace is the area known simply as Topiary, perhaps the most photogenic part of the garden. A double row of box is clipped alternately as simple domes and 'wedding cake' tiers, apparently marching off into the countryside beyond. A line of circular stone stepping stones draws the eye on through the space. The Troughery of stone basins at the house end of the Topiary, also original, is in fine fettle at the moment, overflowing with sedums. A double row of pleached limes (again original) which forms a divide with the terrace proper creates a light contrast to the dark yew elsewhere.

This part of the garden, to the south of the house, remains for me one of the touchstones of world garden design – up there with Vaux-le-Vicomte in France, Thomas Church's Donnell (swimming pool) garden in California, Villa Gamberaia in Florence, the landscape garden at Studley Royal, or Ryoan-ji in Kyoto. I place Rodmarton in such exalted company because the design is possessed of such extraordinary integrity and power, as if every inch of it is being used dynamically to express the character of the place.

The southern edge of the terrace, next to the ha-ha and pasture, is the site of the white borders first introduced by Scrubey in the 1920s (when they would have been novel), which form the beginning of the main east–west axis of the garden. This route takes one past an area of mature trees known as the cherry orchard and the remains of no fewer than three tennis court enclosures. Leisure was a vital component in an Edwardian garden – even an idealistic one such as Rodmarton – and there is a garden room here named the Leisure Garden, originally planted with roses in formal style and now populated with mature shrubs and evergreens planted in the 1950s.

To the north of the main axis, hidden behind the highest yew hedge of all, and the highest brick wall, are the main herbaceous borders, focused at the western end on a small pavilion with a steeply pitched roof in classic Arts and Crafts style. These borders are old-fashioned in the best sense of the word, and superbly maintained – this year the phlox, campanulas and delphiniums in particular were making a great show. There is a small pool halfway along the borders, surrounded by clipped yew topiary which forms little seated areas – again, highly original.

Just to the north is the vast – by today's standards – kitchen garden, a good proportion of which is being kept up skilfully for the purpose it was intended, while a range of specimen fruit trees has been planted in the grassed-over 'outer kitchen garden'.

On my last visit to Rodmarton, a few weeks ago, I was greeted by Simon Biddulph, grandson of Claud, who proceeded to conduct, with great charm and solicitude, a coachload of French garden-lovers around the house interior – he must have given the tour hundreds of times, but it was as if it was the first (professional tour guides, take note). I was enchanted to see, in one of the bathrooms, that the bath contained droplets and the bathmat was wet. Even the grandest house is made to be lived in, and you can't get much more authentic than that. Mr Biddulph's daughter, Sarah Pope, had arranged a sandwich lunch for the French party in one of the buildings in the stable yard, done up very prettily as a sort of café, which was apparently a brand new arrangement. This sort of thing may not be as slick as some operations, but it's what many visitors to historic properties crave. That feeling of the domestic and personal – of authenticity, above all – is what makes Rodmarton so different, and is probably what caused the French to make such delighted gurgling noises.

Daily Telegraph

SUBURBAN MODERNISM
SEPTEMBER 2012

⌁

SUBURBAN MODERNISM (Sub Mod?) is the greatest cliché of contemporary garden design. So many designers – both established and up-and-coming – seem either to work in this milieu or to aspire to it.

Where has this design hegemony come from? Perhaps it's related to the fact that so many tutors in the design schools have made their own real-world design careers out of geometric groundplans, wide decks, expensive-looking furniture, rill-like water features, low rendered walls, timber partitions, big umbrellas and discreetly (or not so discreetly) aspirational barbies and lap-pools. The planting will be grasses, umbellifers (lots of yellow achillea) and *Verbena bonariensis*, with perhaps nepeta, agapanthus or lavender for colour, plus olive trees in pots for an expensive look, or else multi-stemmed silver birches (usually a trio) for a cool Scandinavian slant. The good old 'living wall' or sedum roof is the most recent addition to this portfolio of stock features. Look at the home page of the London College of Garden Design for an excellent example of some of this.

So these tutors want to pass on all their wisdom and experience. But that's a bit like hairdressing tutors of a certain age teaching their students how to re-create Limahl from Kajagoogoo's barnet. As a result, Sub Mod is the look you see repeated every year in the 'sensible' gardens (i.e., the ones without some crazy sponsor's narrative) at Hampton Court and the other lesser RHS shows. When done badly, or shoehorned into too small a space (the usual flaw), Sub Mod can be very 'daytime TV' and very nineties – in fact, the blink of an eye away from the bad dream that was makeover.

It is worrying that this look has been the standard for middle-ranking professional garden design for more than a decade. It screams 'second-rate'. Open that classic of its time *The Essential Garden Book* by Dan Pearson with (we were told) Terence Conran, and just about everything still looks 'up to date' by today's measure. But that book was published in 2001. Have we got no new ideas? Pearson himself has certainly moved on rapidly in the interim, leaving all that bare wood and 'architectural planting' behind him. So why are so many in his wake in thrall to the dead hand of Sub Mod? Pearson recently observed that he was uncomfortable with the idea of his own work being described as 'design', which perhaps reveals more a hint of embarrassment that his work might be bracketed with mainstream garden 'design', which has gone a bit . . . well . . . *show-homey*.

Of course this style stems in part from John Brookes's 'room outside' idea of the 1970s. But we musn't blame Brookes. If you look closely at his work you can see that it was always more about spatial design, architectural patterning and textural interest, and less about 'lifestyle' baggage or being smart. And, crucially, Brookes's gardens never seemed to be getting above themselves by aspiring beyond the space allowed or the neighbourhood in which they were to be found. That instinct came from the socially aware (leftish) origins of Modernism, a nuance which has been all but lost in its transition from idealistic creed into just another design style. In contrast, there is a grandiose savour to much of today's Suburban Modernism – the sense that some of these clients are not just keeping up with the Joneses but screwing them into the ground – and it is fatally undermining.

Wouldn't it be better if new designers were encouraged to look at the precepts of Sub Mod, learn from them (possibly) and then move on? I simply do not buy the argument that this look is just what clients want, and that practitioners have to provide it. There are enough good designers out there to show that it's possible to transcend the hackneyed and the obvious by honing your own style. Suffice it to say that the way designers such as Christopher Bradley-Hole, Cleve West and Pearson deal with smaller spaces is to put a lot of planting in, with minimal but extremely telling 'design' interventions – such as paths, walls and fences or water. It is in planting design that the real advances in British garden style have occurred in the past decade, and most British garden designers are at heart planting designers. I have suggested before that we should play to our strengths. A rule of thumb might be that the less self-evident 'design' there is in a small garden, the more convincing it will be.

Garden Design Journal

This column resulted in an 'apology' from the editor, following complaints from the London College of Garden Design that it had been unfairly singled out for criticism. Below the apology was a statement from TR making it clear he stood by the column as printed.

BEKONSCOT MODEL VILLAGE
SEPTEMBER 2012
↤

WHAT DOES THE AVERAGE ACCOUNTANT secretly want to be? A lumberjack? A stunt motorcyclist? Zsa Zsa Gabor? The truth for Roland Callingham was more prosaic but infinitely more delightful: he became custodian of a miniature village designed for children to enjoy. From its first opening, in 1937, the entrance fee went to charity (the Church Army). What is more, Mr Callingham had built it all himself.

Bekonskot, which celebrates its 75th anniversary this year, is a national treasure, a glimpse of 1930s rural life in miniature which captivates every child who visits it. In those days it was the young Princesses Elizabeth and Margaret who made regular visits to the model village at Beaconsfield – it is not far from Windsor – but generation after generation of children have been entranced by the procession of delights that unfolds as one proceeds in single file round the narrow asphalt paths. Bekonskot is a world packed with incident: there are castles, towns, a fishing port, a zoo, a cricket pitch, a hunt pursuing a fox, an aerodrome, lighthouses, a coal mine, a racecourse and, of course, the longest model railway you have ever seen.

One of the unsung pleasures of Bekonskot, however, is its horticulture, which plays just as important a part in the experience as the model buildings. The overall impression is of manicured lawns and hundreds of dwarf conifers in various shades of green and yellow, crowding round the paths and village scenes. But look closer and you notice that all the evergreens have been carefully shaped and clipped to complement the vistas, and there are even tiny trees with shapely trunks. It is Bekonskot bonsai.

The miniature trees in the village began to be clipped into shape in the 1930s, long before bonsai was fashionable – or, indeed, had even been heard of in Britain. It is not quite bonsai – the trees are planted directly into the ground rather than sculpturally arranged in pots – but the techniques used by the gardeners are the same. 'The good thing about conifers is that you can hack away at them and they can take it,' says Peter Crowther, one of two gardeners at Bekonskot. 'There is not actually such a thing as a dwarf conifer. They call them that, but if you let them grow they behave just like any other tree. These would grow full size.'

Like many gardeners, Mr Crowther is reticent about making great claims for his work, but he is quietly pleased by the look of the miniature deciduous trees, in particular. 'We have quite a few Japanese elms. The leaves are very small and in the winter when the leaves fall off – well, you could call it bonsai.' The Japanese maples, which were planted back in the 1930s and have been kept small ever since, are another highlight, and he is also fond of the oaks – 'In a back garden scene, they can look pretty good.' These trees are really miniature works of art.

It is not all trees. The fine lawns are cut weekly using 1940s bowling-green mowers, for which replacement parts have to be specially made. There is vibrant colour in the form of lavenders, heathers, dwarf narcissi and small irises (like *Iris reticulata*) in spring, and even azalea and rhododendron miniatures. Summer sees the importation of many hundreds of colourful annuals – begonias, petunias, fuchsias and busy lizzies – which make a surreally colourful counterpoint to the traditional scenes of English village life. Then, Bekonskot takes on something of the atmosphere of Day of the Triffids when colourful, bulbous-leaved begonias rear up menacingly behind the players on the cricket pitch.

The focus of this year's 75th anniversary celebrations is on 4 August (the exact anniversary of Bekonskot's first opening), when special activities for children will be laid on. It will be a special day, too, for one Bekonskot employee, eighty-five-year-old Billy Hine, who started work at the model village when he left school in 1931, aged thirteen. Apart from six years away at war, Mr Hine has worked continuously at Bekonskot – for most of that time as head gardener – and he still comes in two days a week.

Daily Telegraph

THE RESONANT ASH
NOVEMBER 2012

⤖

IT WAS GRIMLY AMUSING to read a BBC News online story this week asking, 'Why has ash disease gripped [the] nation's attention?' Among the politically obsessed punditocracy there is apparently something odd and eccentric about the fact people care more about the health of Britain's native trees than, for example, the career prospects of an attention-seeking MP appearing on a 'reality show' in Australia.

There are deep-rooted reasons for people's concerns about the ash. And it's not just about the animals which live in them (measurable ecology also being attractive to newshounds). This tree is a constituent part of the British landscape, its lore and utility deeply embedded in our history. Of our trees, the ash is second only to the oak in national importance; scholars of Anglo-Saxon England might even place it at number one. The resilient and ubiquitous ash, which produces up to 100,000 seeds each year, has always been respected for its benevolent and healing properties. At least three British saints threw their wooden staffs to the ground to see them sprout miraculously into ash trees. Among the rituals associated with the tree is a widespread practice involving the passing of an injured or ill child through a cleft deliberately made in the tree, which subsequently heals over, as does the child. Going even further back, the Vikings' Tree of Life was an ash.

There is usually a utilitarian aspect to such veneration, and ash wood – strong yet flexible – has been used to make ploughs, axles, blocks (on sea and land), planks and latterly all manner of sporting accoutrements, from tennis rackets to oars. Coppiced ash is also unmatched as a super-abundant source of poles. That great historian of woodland Oliver Rackham suggested that some coppiced ash stools 'may be among the oldest living things in Britain (at least a thousand years).' In his *Sylva* of 1662, John Evelyn was enthusiastic about the ash: 'So useful and profitable is this tree (next to the oak) that every prudent lord of a mannor, should employ one acre of ground, to every twenty acres of other land.' Now we know. Evelyn added that as firewood, ash logs are 'the sweetest of our forest-fuelling, and the fittest for ladies chambers'. Aromatherapy *avant la lettre*, perhaps.

Ash has also been a tree of choice for weaponry. In the Dark Ages ash was to the defence of England what the Spitfire was in 1940, for it was used to make spears. The Anglo-Saxon word for ash, *aesc*, also means spear, and is repeatedly invoked in that great poem *The Battle of Maldon*, where the Saxon chieftain Byrhtnoth '*wand wacne aesc*' – 'brandished his slender spear' at the attacking Danes. For their part, the conquering Vikings were known in Britain as the *Aescling* ('men of the ash').

Visually, the ash is our Everyman tree: it can be gnarled and misshapen, lithe and elegant (how Constable drew them), stunted for profitable coppice, or stately and massive (up to 125 feet tall). For a big tree, it does not live long – usually not more than two hundred years – and perhaps for that reason individual ash trees do not generally gain local fame as curiosities or landmarks. But they can be striking features in the landscape, especially when growing as stark, lone specimens in the fields.

For me, the ash has always been resonant, not because of Vikings or saints or spears, but because I grew up with one: a giant (to me) specimen at the foot of our garden, very much of the stately variety. We tend to take big trees for granted in gardens, if we are lucky enough to have them, perhaps because we don't have to 'do' much to them ourselves. But their presence can often set the entire tone – which we suddenly come to realize once the tree dies or is removed. The impact of such a tree is not diminished if it lies in a neighbour's garden – as 'my' ash did. I often found myself gazing into its swirling foliage, mesmerised by its bundles of delicate leaves, brandished aloft like cheerleaders' pompoms, which appear to move in different directions at the same time. And then there's the noise made by all those leaves on an ash tree – something between a hiss and a rush of wind. For a teenager, the tree was a consoling presence.

But now, with die-back, the (literal) decimation of our ash population is a genuine possibility. The spectre of something akin to Dutch elm disease is upon us, the infection spread this time not by beetles but by the wind. Anyone over the age of forty-five will remember the devastation wreaked on elms in the 1970s, and the resulting glaring spaces left in field margins and hedgerows, the felled and rotting trees around our villages. Ironically, it was the ash which largely recolonized those spaces, just as it did in the aftermath of the great storms.

Is it now the turn of the ash? The best hope now, not entirely forlorn, is that this, one of our few native tall trees, might learn to defend itself by developing its own immunity. We can only hope that the ash, a great survivor for millennia on these shores, will somehow survive this challenge as well.

Daily Telegraph, Medlar column

KOREA
AUGUST 2013

Is KOREA the sleeping giant of the gardens world? The venerable history of gardens and designed landscapes of this country has been all but ignored by scholars and commentators in the West, and only partially investigated by Korean writers.

Yet Korean garden culture is in reality just as rich, important and diverse as the traditions of neighbouring Japan and China, which have received far more attention over the years. Korea, after all, has had exactly the same kind of history – of imperial dynasties, monks, bureaucrats, courtiers, teachers, soldiers, poets and scholars, all of whom incorporated garden making as part of the repertoire of what constituted the 'good life'. This overlooked country is replete with interesting historic gardens, ancient temples and dramatic mountain landscapes and, as a result, South Korea is likely to become more of a tourist destination for Westerners, especially as the country continues to soar economically and looms ever larger in our own consciousness – just as Japan did in the 1980s.

I've wanted to visit Korea for many years, and last month, at last, I had the opportunity, thanks to the advent of an international garden 'expo' at Suncheon Bay, at the southern end of the Korean peninsula. I was eager to see how the gardens of Korea compared with those of Japan.

The first thing that struck me on arrival in Seoul was evidence of what I soon realized is a national obsession with trees. It is as if every office block and apartment building in this dense city boasts its own miniaturized version of a forest landscape out front. Valuable street-side real estate has been utilized to create square and rectangular woodland scenes, with mature trees romantically overhanging mosses, ferns and flowering shrubs. These blocks of planting are far more substantial than anything of the kind we might see in Britain, and they frequently evince real character and distinction. In fact there are decorative plantings of trees and shrubs across the city, on almost any available land – like the cloud-pruned trees clustered around and above the entrance to an underground car park, or the native white forsythia which crops up on central reservations. It seems that boundaries are viewed as another excuse for tree planting, as opposed to fencing. And I noticed the way Korean people are able to make gardens out of tiny spaces, with sculpted pines peeping over walls, and flower-crammed containers ranged across steps and window ledges.

Slightly unexpectedly, it was plum and cherry blossom time in Seoul – spring was almost as late in this part of the world as it has been in Britain. In the city's hilltop botanical garden, which has the character of a public park, the bright blossom sang out among the woodland trees ranged up the steep hillsides, thrilling to behold as the dawn light broke. This urban park was full of people all day, while in holiday time Koreans like to go trekking in the mountains in their droves – so much so that there is a serious problem with tracks being worn out in some of its twenty national parks and twenty-two provincial parks. Bukhansan National Park near Seoul has an average of five million visitors per year, reportedly the national park with the highest number of visitors per square foot in the world.

This interest in trees and mountains can be traced back to prehistoric traditions of animism, shamanism, feng shui and the belief in mountain and forest spirits – a religious spectrum known as Seondo. These traditions seem still to exert some residual hold over Korean attitudes to nature. On the vernacular level, there is a 'village grove' tradition in Korea: a revered copse with supernatural qualities at the edge of a village. Animistic beliefs were later incorporated into Buddhist teaching, with almost all the three thousand temples in Korea including a mountain spirit shrine or painting. The oldest traditions of garden making in Korea were concerned with the construction of simple pavilions and walks through unadorned nature, betraying as little human intervention as possible.

Accordingly, it is noticeable how Korean garden and landcape design as a whole tends to be more naturalistic than that of Japan or China. All three traditions include the idea of the miniaturized and idealized landscape – often a mountain scene – translated to the garden setting, but Korean gardens lend as much importance to the sensation of walking through the actual landscape, especially woodland.

You can see this tradition in action at even the grandest of ancient Korean gardens, the Changdeokgung Palace in Seoul, the second most important imperial palace in the city, and the one traditionally most favoured by the royal family. The reason for its popularity rested on its 'rear' or (more cheesily) 'secret' garden, a strictly private 78-acre woodland interspersed with streams, formal pools and pavilions, of which a dozen or so survive today. It was first laid out in 1406 (Korea has a tradition of accurate record-keeping), though the palace complex was later razed several times, either by fire or by invading Japanese forces, and then rebuilt. The steep inclines and elegant winding walks in this woodland 'garden' create the impression that the space is even bigger than it is in reality – at times, it feels like wild nature. Several pavilions are positioned specifically for the enjoyment of tree viewing, while others overlook formal pools with islands.

Away from the rear garden, in the more formal, 'public' palace precincts, there are important garden elements, notably the monumental tiered granite terracing which rises up behind the queen's apartments on three sides, planted with flowering shrubs which are placed so they can be contemplated from the palace's rooms and balconies.

More evidence of the importance of woodland in the Korean imagination can be found at Joseon, the site of the royal tombs on the outskirts of Seoul, a venerated spot which people dress in their best clothes to visit. This is a favoured venue for couples in the advanced stages of courtship (I'm sure I saw one nervous young man proposing; I felt like giving the poor fellow a tot from my hip flask). These monumental tombs, and the grassy precincts which preface them, are all secreted within dense woodland. Other Korean garden highlights are the temples of Seonamsa and Songgwangsa – not too far from the Suncheon Bay expo – and the city of Gyeongju, north of Busan in the south-east, which is to Korea what Kyoto is to Japan: a city of temples and gardens, including a royal palace and the celebrated Anapji pond.

Korea has a climate of extremes, with consistently cold winters, a month-long rainy season (late June and July) and hot, humid summers. As with most places, spring is the best time to visit. Typhoons can hit the southern coast but, unlike its neighbours, Korea is mercifully free of earthquakes. The native flora is extremely rich – British plantaholics may be aware of some of the choicest subjects via the plant-hunting exploits of Sue and Bleddyn Wynn-Jones of Crug Farm Nursery, who have recently brought back Korean delights such as the climber *Aristolochia manshuriensis* (large flowers and stunning yellow foliage); the vivid red, floppy-leaved *Acer buergerianum*; the extraordinary brown-flowered *Clematis flabellata*; very early flowering *Rhododendron mucronulatum* var. *taquetii*; and the startling purple-flowered *Heloniopsis koreana*. Given the fashion for umbellifers (wasn't it the 'Chelsea Cow Parsley Show' this year?), perhaps Crug Farm's Korean cow parsleys, e.g. *Angelica cartilaginomarginata*, might also become coveted by plant connoisseurs.

Since my visit happened to coincide with the latest crisis in North Korea, with dramatic headlines about the imminent threat of thermo-nuclear war in that part of the world, I took roguish pleasure in informing people of my plan to visit the 'demilitarized zone' (the DMZ): four miles of no-man's-land on either side of the border fence between North and South Korea, stretching the entire width of the country. Since this zone is largely untouched by humans and is also riven with minefields and unexploded ordinance, it has become a default nature reserve, hosting a wide range of wildflowers, though perhaps it is the wild animals which are most notable, including the strange, goat-like goral. The weather (torrential rain) and the palpably tense political situation conspired to make my visit to the DMZ rather perfunctory, though I did get some impression of its wildness, behind the wire fences with skull-and-crossbones minefield signs, overlooked by a seemingly endless chain of watchtowers. North Korea has dug four abortive tunnels beneath the DMZ (one of which can be visited: a claustrophobic experience), apparently as part of its invasion plans. Ultimately, however, this idea that the DMZ is a 'nature reserve' struck me as part of South Korea's propaganda campaign to normalize and neutralize the border area.

As for the Suncheon Bay garden expo, this is a vast event which is now attracting up to thirty thousand visitors per day – though hardly any Western tourists. Andy Sturgeon has designed a Modernist show garden in the international area, while Charles and Lily Jencks have created the show's highlight: one of their massive landform projects. Inspired by the Eastern tradition of miniaturizing and visually echoing the landscape, the design honours the tradition of mountain veneration in Korea. 'They do still have this connection to the landscape, which is severed in the rest of the world,' Mr Jencks told me. 'It's a living tradition. They love getting out, walking and wandering. In their hearts they are animists, so they intuituvely relate to everything that grows.' The landform symbolically maps and quotes the surrounding topography by means of seven Jencks-trademark swirling mounds and a central lake representing the city. It occupies the centre of the site and after the expo closes in October will remain *in situ* permanently.

My all-too-brief visit whetted the appetite for closer study and appreciation of Korean garden culture. Who knows, it may end in a book some day. Either way, I shall soon return to this country of mountain landscapes and the subtly picturesque gardens which honour them.

Daily Telegraph

NIGHT GARDENS
OCTOBER 2013
⤫

I HAVE A CONFESSION TO MAKE. Do you remember that television advertisement featuring 'the secret lemonade drinker', the man who raids the fridge in the middle of the night and guzzles fizzy pop? Well, I am a bit like that with gardens . . . the secret midnight garden guzzler.

Every time I go and stay somewhere with a good garden now, I try to experience it at night, and preferably alone. It's almost as if, experiencing a garden in the quiet and dark, it is more likely to yield up its secrets . . . as if it were being caught off guard. This summer has found me communing with the White Garden at Sissinghurst at midnight, inhaling the heady night-time scents of the new wild garden at Gravetye, and assessing the dahlias at Great Dixter without the benefit of glorious technicolor daylight.

The White Garden at night was a revelation, as you might imagine, the rambler *Rosa mulliganii* on the central bower glowing like a lighthouse on a rock, a siren attracting the unwary horticulturist. The yew and box hedging that make up this 'garden room' underpin the scene as they do in the day. Generally speaking it is the form of the garden, rather than the flowers, which comes to the fore in the night garden. Perhaps this is what gives the visitor the impression they are seeing the garden in a more authentic light, as if unfettered. In the White Garden, however, the thrusting yet indistinct spires of white veronicastrum make one understand why white gardens (or grey gardens, as they were first called) were also known as ghost gardens, so mysterious and sequestered they seem. My friend Amicia de Moubray at Doddington Place, in Kent, has been so taken with this idea that she has now made a 'ghost border'.

The night-time garden I know best of all is that of Villa Gamberaia, the great Renaissance garden in the village of Settignano above Florence. Now, this is a garden which all the locals firmly believe is haunted – by the mysterious Romanian Princess Ghyka, who lived there in the late nineteenth century and was rarely seen by day. This does not bother me in the least, for I should quite like to meet the princess. I often enjoy the sublime, rose-festooned water parterre either last thing at night or – rather less often – with the dawn.

That experience brings to mind the account of night-time 'rose parties' which I came across while flicking through a July 1882 edition of the *Gardeners' Chronicle*. 'Rose parties are now being held every day, all day long, and far into the night,' writes the anonymous correspondent. 'Roses by moonlight are something so different in colour and even form as to appear altogether new and different flowers. The perfume, too, is fuller, richer, sweeter . . . the very stillness of the night adds a new charm to the half-revealed, half-concealed beauty of roses.'

Not every night is still, of course, and a lightning storm over Florence this August exhibited the garden at Villa Gamberaia in the most dramatic possible light. Less operatic but potentially just as memorable, a garden will often become agitated by wind during that period from dusk to darkness, an evocative time which can be experienced by visitors who have come for the day. As closing time nears and the visitors drain away, it is easy to find that the garden is 'all yours' in the gloaming. I once met an artist who told me that the direction of her work was changed for ever following just such a late-afternoon visit to the topiary garden of Levens Hall, in Cumbria.

A garden can also be downright discombobulating at night. The most extreme such experience, for me, was a night-time walk through the lakeside formal garden and forest at Middleton Place, South Carolina, first laid out in the 1740s. Here, there is a colony of alligators in the lake, and it is not unknown for them to go walkabout. After dinner, the fifteen-minute stroll from the garden's restaurant to the hotel, in the woods, was rather nerve-wracking, and conducted in my case at an electrifying pace.

But at least the path was lit: pity my poor colleague, the garden photographer who came later to shoot the garden. Working late, she suddenly found the whole place plunged into darkness. She had to walk back through the woods in the pitch dark – a terrifying experience. Relating her close call with the alligators to the staff the next morning, she was assured, 'Oh, it's not the alligators you should have been worried about – it's the snakes hanging down from the trees!'

Daily Telegraph, Medlar column

JELLICOE AT RUNNYMEDE
NOVEMBER 2013
◠

THIS MONTH marks the fiftieth anniversary of the assassination of John F. Kennedy, an event which might prompt some to visit or revisit the landscape memorial to the President, set in woodland overlooking the Thames at Runnymede in Berkshire.

In fact the Kennedy Memorial stone itself is only one element of the remarkable designed landscape realized in 1965 by Sir Geoffrey Jellicoe, Britain's most celebrated twentieth-century landscape architect. It's essentially a walk uphill through woodland, the path emerging at the monumental memorial stone and views back down across the river. But it's considerably more profound than it sounds. The experience is all-enveloping, unfolding gradually over a period of some twenty minutes or so, with the visitor ultimately encouraged to linger and contemplate the historic scene and the great man, what he stood for and his place in history. It's all about movement through space, followed by stillness, a 'memorial landscape' as opposed to simply a memorial.

The visitor begins by walking diagonally across a wide, flat grassy area of pasture on the south bank of the river, following the 'desire lines' left by the tracks of previous pilgrims – I use the word advisedly, since one of Jellicoe's original ideas was for this to be an allegorical journey from the darkness of the woods into the light of the hillside, in the spirit of Bunyan's *Pilgrim's Progress*. The marshy, open-skied meadow at Runnymede was, as every skoolboy kno', where Magna Carta was signed by King John in 1215, an event with obvious significance for a liberty-loving American president. The Thames runs alongside, in one of its pleasantest and most meandering passages, notwithstanding the presence of the always-busy A308 which cuts through the scene (here the visitor fantasizes about having the road diverted to preserve the atmosphere of this historic place, as it is going to be at Stonehenge).

The low, wooded eminence of Cooper's Hill – itself immortalized as an emblem of liberty in John Denham's 1642 poem – rises up to the south, and it is to the woodland edge that the path leads. Passing through a wicket gate, the visitor joins a paved pathway of granite setts, edged with cobbles, which winds uphill and into the woods. This path – which consists of some sixty thousand setts laid directly into the earth – is perhaps the single most noteworthy 'feature' of the design, lending the whole conception a great feeling of unity and coherence, enhancing the sense that one has been absorbed into both the place and the journey through it. For Jellicoe, the setts represented people: the multitude of pilgrims who would find their way here. The winding path is also reminiscent of the one which leads through woodland up to the great Zen gravel garden of Ryoan-ji, in Kyoto. It's probably no coincidence that Jellicoe was commissioned to create this memorial just days before he embarked on his first visit to Japan, during which time he sketched out his initial ideas.

It's quite an arduous little climb up the hill – the effort exerted very much part of Jellicoe's plan – through a self-generating woodland that represents life. As the visitor nears the top, the trees thin while the path straightens up into a series of smooth flagstoned steps leading up to the great memorial stone: seven tons of Portland stone. The smoothness of the steps and the memorial stone itself is in stark contrast with the rough and rugged pathway that prefaces it. The inscription on the stone, carved in monumental capitals, is a quote from Kennedy's inaugural presidental address of January 1961:

Let every nation know, whether it wishes us well or ill, that we shall pay any price, bear any burden, meet any hardship, support any friend or oppose any foe, in order to assure the survival and success of liberty.

Jellicoe insisted that the lettering take up all the available space on the stone – 'so that it is not so much an inscription upon it as an expression of the stone itself; it is as it were the stone speaking.' The stone is shaded by that ancient English tree the hawthorn, with an American scarlet oak planted nearby. Jellicoe wanted it to seem as if these trees were 'in conversation'; he often spoke of trees in the landscape as having a human-like presence.

That is not quite the end of the memorial landscape. Jellicoe did not want visitors simply to turn around and go back down again, so he created another path at a right angle, running west along the contour lines of the hill. This leads to two pairs of steps which take the visitor up to monumental plinth-like benches, with views down across the meadows and river. These contemplative spots were delineated as male and female, though there is no indication which is which. Many visitors do indeed spend quite a long time at this spot, which feels like part of an enclosed feature with a defined purpose, rather than just another resting place on a walk. The walk back down the winding woodland path provides a satisfying sense of conclusion to the experience

The Kennedy Memorial is now in the care of the National Trust, which has plans to create a new visitor centre in one of the twin brick pavilions designed by Edwin Lutyens which flank the road. But the acre of ground itself was originally the gift of Her Majesty the Queen, who formally opened the memorial in the presence of the President's widow and her children in May 1965; in the official document relating to the occasion, there is a photograph showing the Duke of Edinburgh rather touchingly holding hands with the four-year-old John Kennedy Junior as they stand in a line in front of the memorial. The Queen's speech that day was quite political, referring to the shock which left her people 'almost in despair' at the news of the President's death. The wording was strong: 'He was a man valiant in war, but no one understood better than he that if total war were to come again, all the finest achievements of the human race would be utterly consumed in the nuclear holocaust.'

The project was commissioned on the cusp of Jellicoe's epiphanic 'conversion' to Jungian psychology, which caused his later work to become didactic and over-complicated. The Kennedy Memorial can be considered Jellicoe's masterpiece, and it stands as one of the most moving landscape designs in Britain.

Daily Telegraph

MUSEUM WITHOUT WALLS
NOVEMBER 2013
⤎

THE BACK COVER of Jonathan Meades's *Museum Without Walls* proclaims, in large capital letters: 'There is no such thing as a boring place.' What?! Is this guy going to bore the pants off me? I wondered. Reader, my pants stayed largely in position throughout this tumultuous doorstopper (446 pages), mainly composed of journalistic firecrackers about buildings, towns and architects produced over the past twenty years or so, as well as six meticulously scored (though fairly unreadable) television scripts. Meades is a consistently amusing and provocative polemicist and this book is a roller-coaster ride, though not to be consumed all in one go.

Among the things Meades hates most are Tony Blair ('our Christian bomber and his gurning hag . . . the Ceaucescu of Connaught Square'), Albert Speer and the Nazis in general (quite an easy target, admittedly), Libby Purves, Buenos Aires, regeneration ('volume-building in disguise . . . publicly funded parochial vanity'), affordable housing ('there is a significant proportion of the population which cannot afford the affordable'), the Picturesque,

Wayne Hemingway ('his whining, self-pitying, nagging Lancastrian exegeses'), science parks, retail malls, executive homes and the Olympics – 'entirely despicable, entirely pointless . . . a festival of energy-squandering architectural bling worthy of a vain third-world dictatorship, a jobbery gravy train, a payday for the construction industry, a covetable terrorist target'.

It is all richly entertaining, invigorating and provoking; the fearless Meades is to non-fic what Michel Houellebecq is to the good-taste mongers and mutual masturbators of the fic scene. The critic Ian Nairn, the author of *Outrage* (1955) and another great contrarian, is clearly something of a mentor for Meades, who records how he met his hero on two occasions, over 'lunch'. The first time, Nairn drank fourteen pints and ate a packet of crisps. The second time he drank eleven pints but ate no crisps: 'He was thinking about his figure.' In the introduction Meades inveighs against television as only a presenter spurned can, dismissing the management of the networks as a 'cretinocracy'. Meades for his part, now living in Marseilles, perhaps represents the intellectual wing of a chuntering 'croutonocracy' of disgruntled ex-pats.

In common with all modish contemporary writers on outdoor topics, Meades is attracted to ruins, wastelands and 'in-between' places. Thus he traverses the north Kent coast and the pre-Olympics Lea Valley. He likes nothing better than 'polythene bags caught on branches' . . . 'rotting foxes, used condoms, pitta bread with green mould' . . . 'skeins of torn tights in milky puddles' . . . 'soggy burlap sacks, ground elder, a wheelless buggy'. There is a certain poetry to all this decrepitude righteously raining down on us, apparently because of our own crapulousness. In case it feels like we have heard it once too often, Meades is careful to point out that he 'acquired a taste for these marginal places at a tender age'. (Ian Sinclair does not appear in the index.) The towns and cities Meades chooses to write about are similarly compromised, from Tunbridge Wells to Brighton to Portsmouth to Dachau, though he can surprise with a description of the joys of finding fungi, or of finding Birmingham attractive. The best moments in this book come quite randomly, when Meades suddenly hits his stride midway through a peroration, tossing in wonderful new terms like 'psychotic Gothic'.

Meades has the ability to worm his way under the skin of buildings. 'Of London's major set pieces,' he writes, 'St Paul's Cathedral is the most distinguished, though not, I suspect, the most loved: it is too stately, aloof and worldly to excite the sort of affection granted to such exercises in quaintness as Big Ben and Tower Bridge.' But not always of architects: the journalistic profile of Zaha Hadid is disappointingly conventional and gallantly feministic (she is 'nothing if not imaginative').

The author's avowed intention is to suggest, retrospectively, that he has all along been not a buildings boy but a serious commentator on 'the nature of place'. In common with nearly all architectural writers – and until recently architects, too – Meades resists understanding place in its horizontal (landscape) dimension, where there are no clear boundaries and many invisible components, as opposed to its vertical (architectural) dimension, which is entirely bound up with the idea of dominating objects. It's rather like going to the National Gallery, not noticing the pictures, and coming away with the opinion that it's a building with lots of rooms in it. Places, he concludes with uncharacteristic equivocation, 'resist classification'.

During a warm appraisal of John Betjeman ('a pro'), Meades writes: 'The character of a place is to be found in the ordinary – the apparently ordinary. The beans in the cassoulet, not the confit and the sausage.' The major shortcoming of this collection, in the light of its declared theme, is that Meades consistently goes for the sausage of architecture, leaving the beans of place undisturbed.

Literary Review

A CAREER IN GARDEN DESIGN?
MAY 2014

৵

THE BIG QUESTION that anyone embarking on a career in garden design wants answered is, 'What kind of a career path can I expect to follow?' I am sure there are experienced or even seasoned professionals out there who are reading this and thinking, 'Yes, well, actually I'd quite like to know the answer to that one.'

I, for one, don't have the answer, because it seems to me there isn't one. As I noted a few columns ago, this is a 'profession' (or, for some, hobby) which currently operates in quite an ad hoc sort of a way. There is no set career path, with well-trodden byways and intersections which appear at specific moments, as there is in landscape architecture, architecture or any of the more established professions like teaching, medicine or the law.

Going to garden design college is more akin to a spell at drama school, where you are sent forth into the world almost entirely dependent on your own native talent and charm; any financial cushioning you may have; your social status; plus – if you're lucky – a list of pliable friends or contacts who might become clients. I am not saying a garden design course is a waste of time (far from it), but on the other hand, as it stands, it sure ain't a ticket into a professional arena.

It has to be admitted that there is a valid argument against a formal structure. Perhaps it militates against originality? Many established designers of course dine out on their unorthodox entry into the profession and concomitant 'rebel' or outsider status. But for a professional body to take such a laissez-faire stance would be unusual to the point of eccentricity.

As for a pathway, it is possible to gain an apprenticeship of sorts with an established designer, and this is perhaps the very best springboard of all – remembering that the 'best' designers are not necessarily the ones who make the best mentors. Newly qualified designers should be wary, though, of internship syndrome. One landscape architect's office I know has been staffed for years almost entirely by low-paid or unpaid interns, who pass through in their dozens on a revolving door basis, sometimes doing grunt work but on occasion coming up with good designs for which they are able to take zero credit. Seeing them head down at their workstations makes me think of Bob Cratchit.

Then there are the side routes into garden design. The Kew diploma is still the only horticultural qualification truly of international standing, and it has spawned the likes of Dan Pearson, Rupert Golby and Stephen Woodhams (though this is emphatically not a design course). There is landscape architecture (Tom Stuart-Smith, Christopher Bradley-Hole) and art or design school (Sarah Price, Martha Schwartz, Kathryn Gustafson). To be fair, garden design courses did not really exist when most of those mentioned above started out, and they might well have pounced on the opportunity had it been available.

Perhaps because of this vacuum where a career structure ought to be, an excessive amount of importance now appears to be attached to show gardens and awards. It seems that a courtyard garden or other small space at one of the regional RHS shows has become something of a rite of passage for recently (or about-to-be) qualified designers, who are assured this is a good way of getting noticed. They are told that an award will reassure clients that they are bona fide and competent, as they flash a bronze, silver or silver-gilt medal. I'm not sure either of those things is true, and the cynic in me wonders whether it's not an easy way out for the design schools, who want their progeny to feel they are achieving right away.

My own feeling is that within the context of a designer's career as a whole, show gardens are basically worthless. If you look at any books by designers about their own work, the show gardens always look extremely thin and flimsy (in every sense) next to anything at all achieved in the real world. (I would exclude from this sweeping appraisal certain conceptual installations and anything achieved with site-specificity, or in a public place.) A Chelsea show garden might provide a handy injection of cash at the time, but that's not what most designers are in this for, in the end. When I write books about garden design, I hardly ever include images of show gardens, for this reason. They have very little to offer to posterity, however hard designers may find this to swallow.

As for awards, I hate to be the one to say it, but the fact a garden designer has got an award is not necessarily a guarantee of anything. You have to look at the competition. My favourite moment at the SGD awards this year was the Geoffrey Dawes Award, for being Geoffrey Dawes, sponsored by Geoffrey Dawes and presented by Geoffrey Dawes, in which there was one nomination and therefore one winner: Geoffrey Dawes!

Overall, it seems to me that the false 'career path' which has emerged for designers in fact plays into the hands of the organizing institutions and individuals. It may make more sense to steer clear of the system, ploughing one's own furrow, though that does take more guts.

Garden Design Journal (unpublished)

This column resulted in TR being 'let go' from the GDJ *after ten years of monthly contributions. He had already expressed concern that the Society of Garden Designers awards set-up was rather 'cosy' and that little effort had been made to encourage the UK's top designers to participate. This did not go down well at the SGD. But the passage that caused particular offence was the satirical joke about Geoffrey Dawes. For the record, there was no 'Geoffrey Dawes Award', sponsored by Geoffrey Dawes and presented to Geoffrey Dawes by Geoffrey Dawes. In fact, there is also no Geoffrey Dawes: the name of the individual who was the subject of the original joke, a leading committee member at the SGD who was instrumental in setting up its awards and was a regular entrant and winner (though not of the – non-existent – eponymous award) has been changed here.*

PIET OUDOLF IN SOMERSET
AUGUST 2014

✧

THE MOST KEENLY AWAITED new garden to be created in Britain in several years opens to the public next week. The setting is rural Somerset, the designer is Piet Oudolf and the client is international contemporary art dealership Hauser & Wirth. This is already a veritable extravaganza of naturalistic planting design which will in time create a transcendent space for visitors. And it will surely come to be considered an artwork in its own right.

So how did this cutting-edge garden design pop up at an old farm in rural Somerset, on the edge of the small town of Bruton? The story goes that Iwan Wirth, the Swiss co-owner and founder of the gallery, was so enthused by a visit to the High Line in Manhattan that he instantly decided he wanted something similar to adorn his new Somerset base, Durslade Farm, a property he had had his eye on for some time, on land adjacent to his family home. The High Line (in case you didn't know) is an extraordinary linear park that snakes its way across and above New York's Lower West Side, following the tracks of a former freight railway line. Oudolf was brought in to create different naturalistic planting zones and episodes that evoke mood changes as the visitor walks its length – and the effect is mesmeric.

Nothing quite like that can be achieved at Durslade Farm. It's an attractive ensemble of eighteenth-century farm buildings set around a large farmyard which Hauser & Wirth has sensitively converted into a series of rather glamorous gallery spaces (plus restaurant and bar). But the 1.5 acre field which rises up directly behind the farm has been made into something which will potentially create an atmosphere as compellingly other-worldly as the High Line's – once the planting has bedded in, that is. 'It's even bigger than Chicago,' Oudolf comments, referring to his work at Chicago's Millennium Park, lest one should feel like being patronizing about the Somerset location.

I first visited the site, at Oudolf's invitation, in the spring of last year, when it was simply a bare field bounded by a neat hedgerow. We walked the site as Oudolf told me of his concept and then showed me his planting plans (these are currently on show in one of the galleries). Oudolf is a genial figure who is nevertheless given to terse statements about his work. 'We don't try to create nature or re-create nature,' he stated.

I must confess that I was at that point a little nervous about the ground plan: a series of symmetrically arranged planting beds around a central pathway running almost the length of the space, interrupted by raised discs of grass. Yes, it was probably going to be another masterpiece of planting design from Oudolf. But where was the focus going to be? What would anchor the scheme to the space? Oudolf is the world's most influential planting designer, but he is arguably at his best when filling in spaces designed by a landscape architect, as opposed to laying out ground plans himself. With no building or other focal feature at the far end of the space, I felt that this new garden was in serious danger of looking bald and tokenistic.

Returning to the space for an exclusive sneak preview last month, just a few weeks after planting was completed (some 26,000 plants in 175 varieties), my fears have largely been allayed.

The central sandy-gravel pathway that carves through the planting beds does still feel too wide, but the scaling should sort itself out as the plants bulk up. At the bottom of the slope lies an irregular rectangle of a pond, some fifty feet wide, fed naturally by a 'perched' spring further up the hillside. This is invisible until one starts to climb the hill into the garden, subtly and effectively creating a sense of a threshold or gateway into the space.

But the key to this garden, I can now appreciate, is the way it is framed in its setting, rather like a picture in a gallery in fact, by means of the existing hedgerow and by the addition of a series of trees at the foot of the garden. The Kentucky coffee bean tree (*Gymnocladus dioicus*), something of a rarity in itself, has been chosen here partly because of its spreading, horizontal habit. In a few years it will provide a canopy beneath which views of the meadow-like garden on the hillside will open up. The angle of the hillside – the way it seems to be propped up – only enhances the sense that we are looking at a set piece vision, almost an abstract quotation from Oudolf's imagination inserted into the Somerset fieldscape. As he comments: 'It's a real garden – a space enclosed from the landscape – so you feel free to do what you like in there.'

In this context, it does not seem to matter that there is no endpoint to the vista from the downhill, gallery end of the space, where a row of Modernist columns forms a covered terrace with the character of a classical loggia. The strident horizontality of Oudolf's scheme draws you in hypnotically, and I can quite understand why Durslade's head gardener, Mark Dumbleton, says that his favourite way of experiencing the garden is from here.

Something else that had troubled me also now makes sense. Oudolf had specified that very few of the plants in his scheme will grow higher than five feet tall, and that there was to be a general sense of uniformity to the level of planting. Rather than create a monotony as I had feared, this only serves to emphasize the horizontally of the picture he has created, optically foreshortening the view. It enhances the sense that one is seeing the entire composition in one marvellous gulp – which is immensely satisfying. As it happens, this is exactly the technique deployed in the greatest formal Baroque gardens, such as Versailles, though it may seem surprising to see it used in a so-called 'naturalistic' planting scheme like this.

Indeed, it is the plants which are the thing here, as always with Oudolf's gardens. His planting palette favours strong-formed perennials and grasses planted in drifts or – as at Durslade – in clumps, with repeat plantings creating rhythm and unity. The plants are mainly spires such as white persicaria, daisy forms such as rudbeckias and flat-topped umbellifers like sedums. 'Romantic, nostalgic, not wild, organic, spontaneous' is how Oudolf describes his style.

There are several hundred varieties here, but among the stars are orange *Helenium* 'Moerheim Beauty', yellow *Achillea* 'Feuerland',

Echinacea pallida 'Hula Dancer', pink *Lythrum salicaria* 'Swift', *Nepeta govaniana* and the strawberries-and-cream *Sedum* 'Coral Reeves'. The work of Oudolf and his disciples is sometimes criticized for its lack of horticultural interest in the period before September, and a concerted attempt has been made to allay this by means of planned mass bulb plantings for spring, of alliums in almost every species available, plus dramatic *clusiana* tulips, as well as more delicate subjects such as leucojums, *Crocus tommasinianus* and chionodoxa.

This being an art gallery, the plan has always been to sprinkle sculptures across the site, including the gardened areas. By and large this works very well at Durslade – the gigantic metal bucket by Subodh Gupta (now a local landmark) which greets visitors at the farmyard is extremely effective – and Oudolf himself says modestly, 'My garden is there to serve the art.' But I was not persuaded by the decision to place Anri Sala's giant clockface in the middle of Oudolf's design. As I (perhaps rather rudely) said to the gallery director, Alice Workman, 'Would you plant sedums and grasses on top of a piece? Surely Oudolf's intervention is an artwork in its own right?'

Having made this complaint, it has to be said that the cloister created between the farm buildings, where Oudolf has also designed the plantings, is a triumphal marriage of sculpture and planting design. The grasses *Sesleria autumnalis* and *Molinia* 'Moorhexe', plus cimicifugas and euphorbias, rise out of a rough grey aggregate – so suitable to the farmyard setting – that surrounds one of Louise Bourgeois's famed 'spider' sculptures. Another unusual tree has been used here: *Broussonetia papyrifera*, the paper mulberry, an elegant multi-stemmed tree with black fruits which turn bright orange.

'This is a very simple garden,' Oudolf says, referring to the relatively modest (for him) range of plants in the meadow. Perhaps it is simple from his point of view, but I suspect visitors and locals will come to see it as something of a treasure trove.

Sunday Times

The giant clock sculpture was removed from Oudolf's garden.

SHRUBS MAKE A COMEBACK
OCTOBER 2014

THAT STUBBY WORD 'shrub' obscures the fact that this class of plantlife contains some of the most spectacular and beautiful garden subjects of all. The treasures discovered by the intrepid plant-hunters from Kew, despatched to the Chinese forests and mountains in the nineteenth century, were in the main shrubs (familiar plants such as osmanthus, viburnum, rhododendrons and buddleia) – but their often exotic pedigree has been forgotten by many gardeners. For years stereotyped as a lumpen 1970s aberration, the shrub is now determinedly back on trend – though of course for many of the best designers it never went away in the first place.

So, what is a shrub? There is no scientific definition, but broadly speaking the term refers to woody plants which are larger than most herbaceous perennials (also known as 'flowers') but smaller than most trees. In America they refer to them as 'bushes', which is also about right. Roses are shrubs, as are hydrangeas and most plants that can be used as hedging. Some small trees, such as cornus, maples and crab apples, are also classed as shrubs.

What distinguishes shrubs from smaller flowering plants is that their woody stems remain alive and above ground all the way through the year, as opposed to dying back in the winter months. This means that a shrub has a structural presence all year round, especially if it's an evergreen or if its branch structure is attractive. The fact that many shrubs have pretty leaves as well as flowers makes them even more useful to ornamental gardeners.

So what happened to the poor old shrub? The huge interest in flowering perennial plants over the past couple of decades – usually planted in naturalistic swathes in the New Perennials or 'prairie' style – has relegated shrubs to backstage or even offstage. Since the 1990s shrubs have been effectively replaced, in some highly regarded gardens, by the larger species of grasses (miscanthus, molinia and stipa varieties). Grasses can indeed look marvellous in late summer, autumn and even through winter, but after they have been cut back in early spring they can take an awful long time to re-establish themselves. The gardener will have to wait until July or even August for the grasses to come into their own again.

Tom Hoblyn is a Suffolk-based garden designer who trained at Kew, and one of the few designers in living memory to have used massed rhododendrons in a serious Chelsea Flower Show garden. 'When you think about the garden, shrubs should be your next thought, after trees,' Hoblyn asserts. 'We [designers] tried to use grasses like miscanthus, but everyone is going back to shrubs because you can't replace them. I made an experimental border where I used molinia grasses – but in the end I just got fed up with the lack of structure from them and put in five *Hydrangea paniculata* instead.'

Hoblyn, who is currently planting a new garden in Hampshire using hundreds of rhododendrons, observes, 'You can make a whole garden around just one shrub. I love the way they can create a permanent mood. Something like *Aesculus parviflora* [masses of white 'bottlebrush' flowers] has got such a strong character, with that vertical accent from the flowers, almost doing the job of a bamboo. It's like a garden in itself. I would love to have a brief from a client who said, "Please, just use shrubs – no perennials."'

Hoblyn suggests that most shrubs in gardens are drastically over-pruned. 'I very rarely prune roses, for example,' he says. '*Rosa moyesii* 'Geranium' is one of my favourite shrubs. If you let it do its thing, it's like a fountain – a fountain of flowers. And it's got the hips in winter, which birds won't eat unless they are desperate for food. If you haven't got the room, use *Rosa chinensis*. It stays small, it repeat-flowers, it's disease-resistant.'

Among Hoblyn's other favourite shrubby performers are *Chimonanthus praecox* (wintersweet), with lovely delicate yellow flowers, and the 'white forsythia', *Abeliophyllum distichum*, while for smaller gardens he suggests the multicoloured 'heavenly bamboo', *Nandina domestica*. '*Viburnum opulus* is one of my favourite shrubs – if you just let it grow, it will be massive and a little straggly but it will also be a thing of beauty. In gardens I've designed I let it sucker and go mad. Part of their beauty is the sheer volume, so I allow them to romp freely in more naturalistic schemes.'

One of the fastest rising stars of the horticultural world is Tom Coward, who recently took over as head gardener at Gravetye Manor in Sussex. Now a hotel, it was formerly the home of Victorian wild garden guru William Robinson, who was arguably even more influential in his day than his friend Gertrude Jekyll. Like Hoblyn, Coward is Kew-trained, so it is no surprise that he also espouses the naturalistic treatment of shrubby plants in the garden.

'Here we like to present plants in their natural form, because that is what Robinson liked,' he says. 'Something like the weeping pear, *Pyrus salicifolia* 'Pendula', has such a lovely, naturally graceful form. We do prune it a little quite regularly, to enhance its form rather than to control its habit, creating a slightly transparent "skirt" around it. It's terrible when people are too heavy-handed with pruning and basically turn the plants into lollipops.'

The garden at Gravetye includes classic herbaceous borders by the house, a celebrated azalea bank and the remnants of the original 'wild garden' – which is where many of Coward's shrub experiments are occurring. 'Nowadays I am going more towards species plants and single flowers,' he says. 'If we want some bling we can get that from annuals and certain herbaceous material. We're going much more for species roses like *R. moyesii* and *R. rubrifolia* – if they are too hybridized they can jar a little.'

Coward talks of certain shrubs as 'anchor plants', a term he says he inherited from his years working at Great Dixter with the late Christopher Lloyd and head gardener Fergus Garrett. 'At Dixter I learned how you can play off elements of a plant – the foliage, for instance,' he says. 'Some shrubs can get a bit scruffy, it's true, but it's better to have some strong characters in the garden.'

Among the characters currently favoured by Coward is *Clerodendrum bungei* – clusters of pink flowers held elegantly aloft on long stems – because it has good foliage, too, and can even grow in dry shade. Hydrangeas are another recommendation (*paniculata*, *aspera* and *quercifolia* species), 'because you get the flowers in August, which can be a difficult time in British gardens'. He is also particularly interested in leptospermums, exuberant pink-flowered bushes from Australia with good foliage and interesting form, and hawthorns (notably *Crataegus laevigata* and *C. orientalis*), while the red-stemmed willow *Salix purpurea* 'Nancy Saunders' is 'the most beautiful plant and so easy to grow'. But when pressed to name one superstar shrub, Coward names the crab apple *Malus floribunda* 'John Downie', referring to its bright red fruits and white flowers.

Arabella Lennox-Boyd, who has been one of Britain's top garden designers for decades, is known for her love of roses and the way she has melded the romance of English plantsmanship with classic formal designs. Unlike Coward and Hoblyn, Lennox-Boyd is not an advocate of the let-it-all-hang-out school of shrub gardening. 'I like to use things that have a good shape,' she explains. 'Hydrangeas are fantastic – I love *quercifolia* because of the shape of the leaves and for its wonderful autumn colour as well. I also love itea and eucryphias are wonderful. I've got standard Portugal laurels in my own London garden, and a *Cornus controversa* 'Variegata' as the centrepiece, with four or five camellias and a *Magnolia denudata* in one corner. Acers are also marvellous in a smaller garden – 'Acontifolium' is a good one: the leaves are like lace; you can see the sky through them.'

Shrubs used in a more formal scheme do not necessarily have to be the usual topiary suspects like box, beech and yew, she says. 'I use a lot of *Skimmia* x *confusa* 'Kew Green' and *Hebe topiaria* and *H. subalpina* – they are not as formal as clipped box, but almost. What also works really well is the common purple-leaved plum, Prunus cerasifera 'Pissardii', but clipped into a ball. The light coming through the new growth makes it look as if it's covered in jewellery.'

'Some shrubs are sweet and pretty, like deutzia, while others have amazing character – like *Virburnum plicatum* f. *tomentosum*, which I have growing by the lake at Gresgarth, to counterbalance the bridge. I use it as a focal point – just like an urn or a statue.'

Lennox-Boyd recommends good shrubs as the backbone for any London garden, partly because they can better withstand the shade and relative dryness of a typical city plot, and are also low maintenance. But she relishes, too, the opportunity to use shrubs on a large scale, as she has done at the Duke of Westminster's principal seat, Eaton Hall in Cheshire. Here she has planted masses of white *Rhododendron* x *mucronatum* in the spring walk along with other choice shrubs such as the white cherry *Prunus* 'Shirotae' and *Cornus* 'Norman Hadden', which she calls 'the best shrub in the world', with its showers of perfectly sculpted petals.

Variegation is something of a controversial topic among gardeners, with many of those who espouse 'good taste' eschewing such plants altogether. Not so for Lennox-Boyd: 'I'm not mad about variegation but it can be useful in a shady corner,' she explains. 'The variegation has to be very precise and very white; not a yucky yellow colour. I use *Philadelphus coronarius* 'Variegatus' and I grew *Pittosporum tenuifolium* 'Silver Queen' for years. There are also some good cornuses, like *C. alternifolia* 'Argentea'. If it suits the scheme, I'll use it.'

Sally Court is a well-established designer based in Richmond, west London, happy working at any scale of garden, in Britain or abroad. One of her major recent commissions was a three-acre woodland garden at Barvhika, near Moscow.

'Shrubs make for great scenery, with form, texture and presence,' she says. 'It's true that some can become dull lumps, but for example all the different cornus forms are fabulous and there is a viburnum for every season and situation. In Russia we used mainly willows, which grow beautifully over there, plus a lot of cornus and hydrangeas, all of which do brilliantly in semi-shade or woodland. We also planted masses of *Daphne bholua*, for the winter scent and flowers.'

The intention was to create small glades or highlighted moments in the woodland, rather than plant throughout the acreage, a strategy Court has also deployed in the farther reaches of the forty-acre estate at Shalford House in West Sussex. 'It's acid soil there, so we used species rhododendrons and azaleas to create big groves. We also used masses of maples, for the foliage colour,' she says. 'You just can't get the same naturalistic feel using perennials.' This kind of treatment can also work in a town garden – Court has designed a garden in Wimbledon which includes weeping pears clipped formally into pyramids, philadelphus and daphnes, as well as species and modern shrub roses planted at intervals in groups of three.

The lesson from the professionals here is not to be seduced by images of burgeoning borders, and to resist the urge to fill up the garden with herbaceous plants. It is worth remembering that the nursery trade promotes perennials because one has to buy more of them, and more often. The wise gardener invests in trees and shrubs first.

Financial Times

HAUNTED GARDEN
DECEMBER 2014
✑

GHOSTS IN BROAD DAYLIGHT, a curious dreamlike experience, jolts of disorientation followed by the growing recognition that something strange has happened . . . the Trianon adventure, a 'true' Edwardian ghost story, remained a cause célèbre throughout the first half of the twentieth century. *An Adventure*, the book which precipitated the controversy, was a bestseller. Today the story is almost forgotten, yet it retains a curious resonance for anyone interested in gardens and their particular atmospheres.

The 'adventure' in question happened on a hot day in August 1901, when two academic ladies, Anne Moberley and Eleanor Jourdain, paid a visit to Versailles and the *jardin anglais* of the Petit Trianon

– Marie Antoinette's celebrated hideaway half a mile to the north of the main palace. This is an informal landscape of mazy paths, meandering streams, dark glades and small, evocative buildings, such as the Temple of Love (a neoclassical rotunda), the Belvedere (an exquisite octagonal pavilion) and the adjacent Rocher or rock bridge. Secreted in a cleft among the little knolls behind the Belvedere is the Queen's Grotto, a delightfully discreet little feature with entrances on two different levels; it was here that Marie Antoinette was reputed to have been found, deep in thought, when she was first told of the mob's approach. The planting in the garden was restored in 2008 using a 1795 botanical inventory, including numerous specimens of what were then North American rarities. But even today, perhaps the chief sensation this garden inspires is disorientation.

Miss Moberley was principal of the fledgling all-female Oxford college St Hugh's, and Miss Jourdain was headmistress of a girls' school in Watford. The two were spending three weeks sightseeing in Paris, partly in order to assess their compatibility as potential colleagues at St Hugh's.

According to Miss Moberley and Miss Jourdain, that afternoon they encountered a succession of people in late-eighteenth-century costume, some of whom spoke to them. At the time they thought little of it, though they later concluded they must have been ghosts. The first of these spectres was a servant woman shaking a sheet from the window of a building (later found to be non-existent), followed by a pair of ill-mannered 'gardeners' in uniform (subsequently identified by the ladies as Swiss Guards), then a repulsive-looking man with a pockmarked face leaning on a balustrade next to a rocky outcrop. He was followed by a handsome, out-of-breath young man in a wide-brimmed hat, who appeared as if from nowhere behind them and told them to go back to the palace immediately. The climax of this ghostly tour was a woman seen sketching (by Miss Moberley only, although in later testimony Miss Jourdain said she could sense a presence) who could only have been Marie Antoinette herself – at least, that is what the ladies claimed.

After much research in the archives, their eventual interpretation of all this was that they had somehow entered a daydream of Marie Antoinette's while she was imprisoned in Paris in 1792, as she remembered her final day at the Trianon in 1789. The ladies suggested that they had gone back in time and participated in this reverie, and at one point even occupied the body of the queen herself – why else would they have been urged by the handsome servant to return to the palace?

One of the many extraordinary features of the story was the ladies' later insistence that, at the time, neither of them remarked upon the fact that anything unusual was happening to them. They noticed the strange costumes, they said, but reconciled them to modern life in different ways. It was only several months after the event that they began to suspect that they may have had a paranormal experience, and wrote down their testimonies. It transpired that they did not see exactly the same things at the same time, and a second visit to Versailles by Miss Jourdain revealed that the topography of the place as they remembered it was in fact quite different: certain features had disappeared entirely or been replaced by others; paths had vanished; distances seemed radically foreshortened. In addition, Miss Jourdain had some more ghostly sightings: peasant labourers loading a cart at the Hameau (Marie Antoinette's model farm, adjacent to the Petit Trianon), a tall man walking through the woods, and the sound of music.

These delays and discrepancies were subsequently to provide ammunition for sceptical observers, but they also lend the story a peculiar piquancy, a frisson of the random unexpectedness and odd detail of real life, that has proved irresistible to many readers. Reading the ladies' accounts, one cannot help but be carried along by the story, whether or not one believes it is true. With their book, Miss Moberley and Miss Jourdain produced an accidental masterpiece of supernatural fiction.

An Adventure was not published until 1911, almost a decade after that spectral afternoon at Versailles. The ladies felt compelled to tell their story – albeit under pseudonyms – because of the short shrift they had received from the Society for Psychical Research, to whom they had sent their accounts in 1902. The scepticism of the society infuriated Miss Moberley and Miss Jourdain, and they embarked on a concerted, even obsessional, campaign of research in the French national archives and elsewhere, aimed at positively identifying the various characters and buildings they had seen. This they did – and they believed triumphantly so – although in fact the evidence they present in the various editions of their book is, to put it kindly, far from conclusive. But the ladies continued to be taken seriously because of their social and academic respectability: no one could quite believe that they had simply made it all up.

After all, both were Christian ladies of high reputation. Miss Moberley, then in her mid-fifties, was the daughter of the late Bishop of Salisbury, for whom she had acted as secretary for twelve years, before being selected as first principal of the new Oxford college. Miss Jourdain, in her late thirties and also the daughter of a clergyman, was another powerful personality. What was not widely known was that they already had a mutual interest in visionary experience – albeit religious as opposed to 'supernatural'.

So what was the truth? Of course there is a chance that the ladies really saw the ghosts, but it seems more likely that between them they embroidered their memories of events, then talked about them publicly, and finally found they had no choice but to justify the stories as they best knew how – through academic research. Once that decision had been taken, there was no going back: their reputations, and also that of St Hugh's, were at stake. It is possible that the ghosts may have been real people wearing eighteenth-century costume, dressed up for a *fête champêtre* or for a film, or perhaps as guests at one of the parties which were known to have been held around this time at the Petit Trianon by the dandyish Comte de Montesquiou. But there is no conclusive evidence for any of this.

I am inclined to believe that the ladies invented almost everything on the slenderest basis from actual experience, partly arising from their own readings around the subject, as a manifestation of their excitement and delight at having met each other at all. After their meeting in Paris, Miss Moberley and Miss Jourdain remained devoted companions, referred to as 'man and wife' by the college servants. Close attachments between women were common among those in charge of these early female educational establishments. Paris was then the epicentre of such sexual emancipation, and Marie Antoinette was something of a cult figure. In the end, the Trianon adventure is perhaps more of a love story than a ghost story.

Daily Telegraph

ALICE
FEBRUARY 2015
⟿

I HAVE BEEN SEEING ALICE EVERYWHERE. Not just because it's the 150th anniversary of the book's publication – nothing to do with that in fact. Alice is in my thoughts because I have been spending a great deal of time in Oxford college gardens, the title of a book I have just finished writing. Alice is everywhere in them.

The Deanery Garden at Christ Church – Oxford's 'cathedral college' – was where it all started. Charles Dodgson (Lewis Carroll) was a lecturer there in the 1850s when he was charged with cataloguing the library's books. From his little office at the back of the grand eighteenth-century library building, he had a good view down into the Deanery Garden, where the Dean's children, including Alice, would play. This garden is hidden from view today as it always has been, a long wall dividing it again from the cathedral and its garden. It was a wooden door in this wall which tantalized Alice as a young girl, because it was kept locked and she was always told it was out of bounds. The whole story of Alice is based on her attempts to get into just such a secret garden. Even her father the Dean – the college principal – was not allowed through this door, and had to go the long way round to get to the cathedral. This meant he was often late. The White Rabbit's panicked, 'I'm late! I'm late!' is supposedly a reference to Dean Liddell's comical fluster.

A horse chestnut tree, with a great horizontal bough, which still stands in the Deanery Garden, is reputedly the one in which the Cheshire Cat sat, just as Alice's own cat, Dinah, did. The Red Queen's croquet match in *Alice in Wonderland* was probably Dodgson's satire on this new game which was taken so seriously by its participants (he was able to watch them play from his eyrie in the library). The real Queen Victoria paid a state visit to Christ Church during Dodgson's time, but the Red Queen herself was based on the Liddell children's fierce governess, Miss Prickett. Finally, the Mad Hatter's tea party was purportedly based on one of Alice's own birthday parties, held in the Deanery Garden.

Oxford is notoriously a 'bubble' for the fellows of colleges, and Dodgson perhaps inevitably located parts of the story in settings derived from the Oxford gardens he knew so well. Alice is actually a rather bucolic tale, with far less happening indoors than outdoors. And the landscape and river described is recognizably that of Oxfordshire.

After Dodgson had made friends with Alice and her sisters, he would take them on boat trips – including the one in July 1864 when he told the Alice stories for the first time – and also on visits to college gardens. A long subterranean passageway at Worcester College may have inspired the rabbit-hole down which Alice first falls. There is a real treacle well, too: it was the name locals gave to St Frideswide's Well at Binsey, because of its healing properties – it was a place Dodgson visited with Alice.

Perhaps the biggest clue to the strange, shape-shifting landscape of Alice is the city of Oxford itself, as it performs various optical illusions on the visitor. For example the city viewed from the river bank, across Christ Church meadow to the south – whence Alice and company embarked on their boat outings – looks far larger and more distant than it really is, the 'dreaming spires' apparently a mythic land.

Narrowing the focus, Christ Church itself, Dodgson's home, is possessed of a layout and architecture that almost seems designed to disorientate, swelling and receding and – crucially – making the human being feel very small indeed. Tom Quad is impossibly large, while neighbouring Peckwater Quad introduces an equally grand but subtly different sense of scale. The result is that it feels as if you are in an architectural model. Time is disordered at Christ Church, as well: Tom Tower's chimes deliberately do not keep time with the rest of Oxford's bells.

The moment when one leaves Christ Church, through its grand back door, the Canterbury Arch, is positively surreal, with the scale suddenly miniaturized to suit the higgledy-piggledy houses of Oriel Square. Perhaps the view from the gate down Merton Street, with the entrance to Corpus Christi like a hole in the wall on the right, gave Dodgson the idea for the long corridor with the tiny door in which Alice first finds herself.

These actual places, which Dodgson knew so well, have an effect on the visitor which is reminiscent of the way one feels reading the book. Part of Dodgson's sublime genius is the way he makes this fictional world seem so strangely plausible, and perhaps that is because it was quite real to him.

One last thing. While preparing this column I was looking through materials about Alice and was shocked to find a photograph by Julia Margaret Cameron of Alice aged twenty-one, framed by hydrangea flowers. It is familiar to me because a print of it – which I picked up I cannot remember where – has been propped on the mantelpiece in my bedroom for the past dozen years. I don't know why it appealed, and I have not known until now who the subject was.

It seems that whilst I have been watching out for Alice, all along she has been watching me. How very Alice.

Daily Telegraph, Medlar column

A LITTLE CHAOS
MARCH 2015
～

THERE IS A MOMENT in *A Little Chaos* – Alan Rickman's new film about a feisty female garden designer (Kate Winslet) – in which King Louis XIV, played with imperious gusto by Rickman himself, pays a visit to a tiny enclosed fruit garden at Marly. Here we discover an elderly gardener, bewigged like everyone else in the film, pottering about and savouring his pears – 'my little beauties', he mutters.

At this point I suddenly thought, 'No, it isn't ... it can't be ... can it be?' And then a liveried royal servant whispers in his ear, 'Monsieur de la Quintinie –' before whisking him off to see the king.

It was true. The film was actually name-checking Jean-Baptiste de la Quintinie, the man who created the Potager du Roi in the 1680s, and who wrote one of the greatest ever books on fruit and vegetables. I had to struggle to control my excitement at seeing this figure of garden history made flesh, as he stroked his ripe pears – which would surely have been 'Bon Chrétien', though the film did not quite go so far as specifying the variety. (If it had, I would probably have sunk to the floor and joined the popcorn.)

This little vignette is one of the many pleasures – for gardeners – of a film which celebrates gardens and their history in a way which no other does. Yes, we have had films such as *The Draughtsman's Contract* (1982), which used Penshurst Place as an evocative backdrop, but *A Little Chaos* is squarely and actually about gardens and garden design.

The film begins with Winslet, playing the fictitious designer Sabine de Barra, buying a ridiculous hat to wear for a job interview with André Le Nôtre. Not the great Le Nôtre Senior, creator of Versailles, but his son, played by Matthias Schoenaerts, who is – I am given to understand – rather dishy in a Belgian sort of a way. (One can't quite imagine him as a gardener – though admittedly his immaculate designer stubble must require some careful cultivation.) The 'little chaos' of the title is signalled by the Winslet character surreptitiously moving a pot at the centre of Le Nôtre's own garden, thereby disrupting its formal symmetry. Never mind that Le Nôtre himself had already experimented with naturalism at Marly – this is cinema.

After a predictably rocky start, an equally predictable romance develops between the two, as Winslet struggles to complete her assignment: the creation of the Salle de Bal, or water ballroom, as one of the bosquets situated in the woods that flank the Great Canal at Versailles. Again, it is marvellous that an actual garden feature is accurately depicted.

Not all of the garden history is spot on – there are a number of plants (including astilbes and brugmansias) in Winslet's own little garden which were not in cultivation in Europe in the late seventeenth century – but one does get a sense of the mud and hard engineering work involved with the creation of a water feature of this scale and complexity. For her part, Winslet revealed that her research for the film consisted of gardening – 'getting my hands dirty ... there would always be little bits of mud somewhere or other.'

Rickman obviously delighted in playing the king – an unexpectedly sympathetic portrayal of an essentially lonely man – and the supporting cast includes Stanley Tucci playing against type as the homosexual Duc d'Orléans (his amusingly mannish wife taking an interest in Winslet). The rituals of the French court are particularly well done, with much décolletage in the bocage. The most touching and delicate scene in the film is a quick-fire conversation 'backstage' at court where our gardener discovers a strange sense of community with the ladies of the court, as they talk of transactional marriages and the children they have lost. One elderly aristocrat relates how her husband and son were both killed on the battlefield on the same afternoon, quietly concluding, 'I am barely here.'

Not everything in this cinematic garden is lovely, however. While there are some convincingly intimate scenes involving Winslet and Rickman, the chemistry is not quite there between the romantic leads, with Winslet's gardener permanently stricken because of a 'terrible secret' which haunts her. We discover the truth about this just before the film's grand finale, which is the unveiling of the Salle de Bal itself. In a final coup de horticulture, the garden is allowed to steal the show, as Rickman and Winslet dance in front of the cascade and the all-too-palpable magic of CGI whisks us up and away above Versailles.

Film critics will dislike the stately pace of *A Little Chaos*, and it is certainly let down by its romantic interest – so this will probably be adjudged only a three-star effort for a general audience. For readers of this section, though, it has to be five stars. This is a ripe and juicy pear of a gardener's film, with much to sink one's teeth into. Catch it while you can, as I have a feeling it will not be on general release for long.

Daily Telegraph

ON ISLANDS
APRIL 2015
↜

WHAT IS IT ABOUT ISLANDS? Having just returned from a week's walking and botanizing on Madeira, I have to say there is nothing like a dose of island life to refresh the senses and revitalize the vitals. And, like islands, gardens are considered to be 'transcendent' spaces: other worlds where normal rules do not apply. The triple whammy of island, garden and holiday is surely hard to beat.

Gardens on islands often take advantage of the unique microclimate or topography of the place. In the case of Madeira, the verdancy of the plantlife is generally attributed to the rich soil that results from the island's volcanic history – though I note that the most recent book on the topic suggests that this is a myth and that the stony soil needs to be coddled. Madeiran gardens are eclipsed anyway by the island's wildflowers, which can be seen in profusion along the *levada* (canal-side) paths which penetrate the mountains. These walks, which skirt sheer cliffs with no handrails and pass through long tunnels, are astoundingly beautiful but famously vertiginous. I must confess that at one point – as my wife and children dashed across a ledge through a drenching curtain of waterfall with a 150-foot drop just inches away – I did think to myself, 'Whose bright idea was this?' My nerves were soothed by the sight of a group of echiums coming into flower, of a species endemic on Madeira, a little farther along the path. Island plants are often special cases.

Another fine island destination for garden lovers is Lanzarote. The architect César Manrique, who was born on the island, created a number of gardens on its harsh black volcanic rock – including a remarkable botanical garden for cacti and succulents, in a crater. He also designed quite the coolest nightclub I have ever seen, submerged in a deep cavern filled with hanging plants.

Some islands, such as Tresco in the Scilly Isles, become defined by a garden which has been made there, while the baroque confection of Isola Bella on Lake Maggiore in Italy completely subsumes its island. A fine garden on an isolated or remote island can be a fine surprise, as with the garden made by Edwin Lutyens and Gertrude Jekyll for the editor of *Country Life* at Lindisfarne Castle, in Northumberland. Sometimes an island garden is a sideshow which must be sought out: the quality of the cliffside garden at St Michael's Mount in Cornwall often takes people by surprise.

On a smaller scale, islands can be an intriguing addition to a garden's design. Such features were popular in the eighteenth century – the most celebrated garden island of this period is the atmospheric Isle of the Poplars at Ermenonville in France, on which the philosopher Jean-Jacques Rousseau was buried. In Britain, the magnificent (recently restored) grotto at Painshill in Surrey is on 'Grotto Island', while nearby Claremont landscape garden boasts William Kent's Belisle pavilion. The island in the lake at West Wycombe Park is the setting for a Music Temple which is modelled on the Roman Temple of Vesta (which was not actually situated on an island – but who cares?)

With garden islands, part of the fun is in the getting there. The exhibits in the contemporary Hortillonages festival in Amiens, northern France, can only be reached by means of electric-powered boats, steered by visitors themselves around a huge, island-studded lake. But water can also mean trouble. The Scottish gardener Thomas Blaikie, who ended up as head gardener to Marie Antoinette, relates in his diary the visit of the Grand Duke and Duchess of Russia to the garden of the Comte d'Artois, who was then his employer. The unfortunate Russian ambassador, eager to take the hand of the Duchess as she progressed to the hermitage, slipped, tumbled down a bank and fell into the lake. Blaikie reports that this gave rise to a good deal of laughter from the Queen and others present, with which he joined in, 'although obliged to hide'.

Daily Telegraph, Medlar column

LONG BARN
MAY 2015
↮

ALWAYS THE BRIDESMAID, never the bride – that has been the fate of Long Barn, the garden in the Kentish Weald that Vita Sackville-West and Harold Nicolson made before they came across a certain semi-derelict castle and created what is probably the most famous garden of the twentieth century. But Long Barn has its own magic. It would certainly be more celebrated were it not perpetually in the shadow of its more glamorous sister.

Harold and Vita bought the gloriously misshapen fourteenth-century house in 1915 and lived there for fifteen years, honing both their gardening and their design skills. According to their son Nigel Nicolson, 'The floors sloped crazily, so that every piece of furniture appeared crippled, and the roof was held together less by construction than by natural angles of repose. In place of a garden there was a chute of rubble and a tangle of briars and nettles.'

The sixteenth-century 'long barn' itself was moved up the hill to its current position next to the house and transformed into a fifty-foot-long sitting room giving on to a square-ish terrace. From here, the garden gently falls away to the south, with fields and woodland beyond. The most striking element is the avenue of twenty mature clipped Irish yews which creates a dynamic east–west axis, but lawns on the wide terraces mean that overall the impression is not of a garden of 'rooms', despite an underlying cellular structure.

Vita later reminisced, 'I myself took to gardening quite late in life. I must have been at least twenty-two.' In fact she was twenty-three when she arrived at Long Barn. She and Harold dived in with gusto, he ordering plants from nurseries and she making horticulture a pendant to her writing life. In one letter to Harold, in 1926, she is ecstatic about her 'wood garden', as she called it, using the word 'alive' repeatedly. Later that year Harold wrote to Vita, inveigling against rhododendrons (then in fashion), specimen trees and in fact all non-natives except flowers: 'You see, I think our stunt at Long Barn is to keep the Kentish farm background, and in that background to embroider as much as we like.' These are the same ideas which came to inform Sissinghurst.

Long Barn has its own character, then – something Nigel Nicolson dubbed 'an atmosphere of fourteenth-century rusticated innocence' – and this has been revealed and enhanced since 2007 by the current owners, Lars and Rebecca Lemonius, who employ two gardeners (one full-time). The style is romantically soft and effervescent, with Mrs Lemonius stating: 'It's loose – but I don't want it too loose. I want to keep it looking natural without it becoming a mess.'

The key to this tone lies with self-seeding or spreading plants, including the white umbellifer *Ammi majus*, daisy-like erigeron and feverfew, yellow santolina and helichrysum, vivid purple *Campanula portenschlagiana* (in the walls), glaucous *Artemisia* 'Powis Castle' and an un-named plum-coloured poppy sourced from a Dutch garden. Roses are another staple, with varieties including 'Tuscan Superb', 'Madame Alfred Carrière', 'Prospero',

'Valentine', 'William Shakespeare' and 'Munstead Wood'. Earlier in the season irises such as 'Jane Phillips' and 'Black Swan' take centre stage, while dark penstemons (notably 'Raven' and 'Garnet') also play their part.

The brickwork terrace is a classic suntrap and has been a favourite sitting place for generations of owners. Today it is enlivened by a large *Fremontodendron* 'California Glory' that grows against the barn wall. A path extends eastwards above the lawn, accompanied by clipped balls of box and hebe, and masses of purple verbascum. At the far end of the barn is a box parterre (a rather 1980s feature today enlivened with big grasses) and then, leading north and upwards, a scented rose walk with twisted-hazel arches.

Just below the main lawn, on another wide terrace, is the Pleasaunce Lawn, with a small formal pool enclosed by hedges at its western end. As Mrs Lemonius reflects: 'If you terrace you naturally start to create garden rooms.' The herbaceous beds here contain one or two more unusual plants, including *Triteleia laxa* 'Ocean Queen'.

The Dutch Garden, occupying the largest and lowest terrace, was reputedly laid out by Edwin Lutyens – and it does express a certain spatial confidence. Today the six raised beds are the proverbial 'riot of colour', with clematis, daylilies, ligularia, alliums, roses, phlox, poppies, geraniums, diascia, sedums, aquilegias, echinops and veronica (including *V. austriaca* 'Crater Lake Blue'). An underlying order is maintained by the geometry of the beds and corner plantings of white-flowered Korean hill cherry (*Prunus verecunda*).

East of the compartmented areas the garden dissolves into more informal spaces: an ex-tennis court which is now the Rose Lawn, an old orchard (with more roses, and snakeshead fritillaries and orchids in spring), and the Classical Grove, with statuary set amidst trees and long grass and a small pond – formerly the swimming pool. Immediately south of the house are two small gardens: a white garden and a new sloping spring garden designed by a student from KLC School of Design.

Yes, one can play the game of looking for features which seem to anticipate Sissinghurst – but the garden at Long Barn deserves so much more than that. Pocketed in the Wealden countryside, it creates its own psychological microclimate.

Gardens Illustrated

CHELSEA FLOWER SHOW

MAY 2015

QUESTION: when is a garden not a garden? Answer: when it's a trout stream. The question arises because the show garden that is most hotly tipped to win the top accolade at Chelsea Flower Show next week is the Laurent-Perrier Chatsworth Garden, designed by Dan Pearson (the plantsman commissioned to work on the Garden Bridge).

The design is based on a re-creation of a slice of the great Derbyshire estate – teleported, as it were, into the Royal Hospital showground. The planting around it is being designed to look as natural as possible, with the hand of the designer barely figuring. It's all very much in line with current trends in planting, which look to the way plants disport themselves in nature for inspiration. At his own new farmhouse property near Bath, for example, Pearson is not 'designing' the garden as such but managing it as a small estate, with a light touch and no visible decorative flourishes. According to this slightly cultish fashion, we don't have gardens nowadays – we have 'plant communities'. Insects are not pests to be eradicated, but 'wildlife' to be cherished and conserved. Percy Thrower must be turning in his grave.

Aside from the obvious speculation as to whether this trout stream will be flowing with sponsor Laurent-Perrier's champagne, it does rather beg the question as to whether it fits the Chelsea bill. Is it a garden? After all, the Royal Horticultural Society rules state that a design must be imaginable as a 'back garden' somewhere. And not many of us could imagine having a garden that is a trout stream. I suppose one could argue that the Chatsworth estate is de facto the back garden of the Duke and Duchess of Devonshire, and that this show garden is a small portion of it, but that does seem to be pushing it a bit, even in the slightly rarefied atmosphere of Chelsea Flower Show, where dowager duchesses in battered Husky jackets jostle with high-heeled bankers' wives for a view.

Now, I am not one of those who bemoans the way Chelsea bears no relation to 'real-life' gardening. I don't go to Chelsea for that. I go for the fantasy, and for the best displays of the art of horticulture on the planet. If home gardening is street fashion, then Chelsea is haute couture. If I want an old garden hose and some empty pots, I can stay at home. But at the same time I do wonder whether a slice of natural landscape has very much at all to do with horticulture, at a show which is after all organized by the august RHS. Last year's Chelsea had so much of the hedgerow about it that it might just as well have been the 'Chelsea Cow Parsley Show'. And to judge by the planting lists circulated by the 2015 cadre of designers, this time around it could be the 'Chelsea Foxglove Show'.

The emergence of the trout-stream-as-garden is possibly indicative of a loss of a sense of direction among the show's organizers, following a string of slightly uninspiring Chelsea shows in recent years (the nadir, ironically, being the centenary year in 2013). There is now no clear identity for Chelsea show gardens. It used to be that they were essentially display gardens along the Ideal Home Show model, replete with practical ideas which householders could use. Or else they were glorified nurserymen's showcases – especially for rhododendron and azalea growers – though the RHS put a stop to that a few years ago when they abolished the showground's 'Rock Bank', traditionally the home of these dated extravaganzas.

At some point in the mid 1990s, the old display garden model began to give way to a variety of other approaches. Chic Modernist designs became de rigueur after a particularly successful example 'won' the show in 1997 (I remember it well, because that year I was managing the next-door garden, a much more traditional number sponsored by *Country Life* magazine). Symbolic designs – often conceived as 'journeys' from darkness to light – became the preferred option of the charities who like to sponsor gardens because of the guaranteed TV coverage. This odd sub-culture of garden design was extended into the realm of finance, as the banks and investment houses – which have long favoured the Chelsea show as a place to entertain clients – developed their own kind of symbolic garden, with horticulture used to embody the concept of 'investment in the future'.

Anyone who is seriously interested in gardening knows that you don't visit Chelsea to see the best structural and spatial garden design, given the almost impossible brief handed to designers – a double whammy of RHS rules and sponsors' demands. It's the planting which matters, and Chelsea remains the best barometer of connoisseurial planting style in the world. Whatever the RHS says publicly, the judges make their awards on the basis of the texture, tone and sophistication of the plantings, with marks deducted for particularly egregious examples of sculpture or 'water features'. This bias has meant that most Chelsea designers have since the 1990s increasingly conceived of their designs as vessels for planting beds, with far more space given over to this aspect than there would be in any real garden.

More recently, the ecological concerns currently besetting us have been echoed in Chelsea show garden design (lots of green roofs, water recycling and 'rain gardens') though there is far less of that this year. In its place we have the concept of the community garden influencing Chelsea design, with both Morgan Stanley and Homebase jumping on that bandwagon for marketing purposes – though there is precious little evidence that they are supporting such activity out in the real world.

And tucked in amidst all of this as a constant are the unapologetically romantic English cottage gardens – which always win the 'people's choice' award – and the 'foreign' gardens sponsored by tourist boards, wineries and luxury property companies. The latter usually fall down on planting quality but add a welcome note of exotica (the most exotic of all was the 'Martian' garden which won Best in Show in 2007).

The truth is, I don't think that Dan Pearson's Chelsea garden is going to look much like a real trout stream at all. He will want to secure a gold medal for the sponsor, and will therefore create a subtle extravaganza of planting with a naturalistic feel to wow the judges. As a result he still has a good chance of scooping the top prize. Chelsea Flower Show is a game, and the designers are playing to win.

Evening Standard

FROM VERSAILLES TO POPLAR
MAY 2015
✧

HOT ON THE HEELS of *A Little Chaos* – the sumptuous Versailles-set extravaganza starring Kate Winslet and Alan Rickman – comes another British-made film which takes gardening as a central theme. Based on actual events which unfolded with horrific alacrity over ten weeks in late 2006, *London Road* is a film adaptation of the National Theatre hit show which follows the story of a group of Ipswich neighbours whose lives are turned upside down by the murders of five women in the city. (It turned out that the murderer was renting a house in London Road at the time.) The film obviously has a flavour very different from that of the Winslet/Rickman escapist fantasy, but in the event gardening proves just as important in the lives of the benighted Ipswich residents as it does for the Sun King.

Admittedly it's a pretty grim premise, with the first two-thirds of the film played out against an unremittingly greyed-out backdrop of Ipswich's streets, where the town's traumatized and frightened residents eye each other with mutual suspicion. *London Road* is not a film in which to lie back and bathe – as *A Little Chaos* is – but it is compelling in its own way, largely because it was conceived as a musical with a documentary feel. This means that everyone in it, from newsreaders to teenagers to ghoulish crime-scene tourists, delivers staccato singsong lines which have been culled verbatim from real interviews and footage, complete with 'ums' and 'ers'.

After about an hour of relentless tragi-musical mock-doc, I was beginning to wonder whether any gardening was going to happen. But of course the plot follows the classic narrative-arc formula: a dip just past midway followed by a life-affirming 'third act'. Suddenly the residents start to pull together under the leadership of matter-of-fact Julie – played by native East Anglian Olivia Colman. A London Road in Bloom competition is announced because, as Julie reasons: 'If you feel good about your house and where you're living, you'll enjoy life more.'

The film's colours suddenly warm up, in the manner of *The Wizard of Oz*, as hanging baskets in glorious technicolor are planted, decks laid, lawns mown and windowboxes stocked with jolly annual flowers. The song 'London Road in Bloom' – a list of flowers recounted by all the residents – is one of the most affecting numbers, symbolic of the way the residents have reclaimed or cleansed their neighbourhood. The characters we have come to know as forlorn and stuttering interviewees in their front rooms are suddenly re-energized as horticulturists, happily describing the 'begonias, impatiens and things . . . petunias' which they are growing.

London Road taps in – probably quite accidentally – to something of a zeitgeist in the horticultural world. Community gardens have become a phenomenon across Britain in the past few years, and not just in urban areas (I was surprised to find one in an affluent Home Counties village recently). Everyone knows about the surge of interest in allotments over the past decade or so, with long waiting lists in some urban centres, but equally we have become aware of the way this trend has fallen off recently, perhaps as the demands of allotmenteering have hit home to twenty- and thirty-somethings trying to earn a living or start a family.

Now we have growing interest in community gardens – a much sturdier proposition, potentially. There is a new generation of gardeners out there, defined by their attitude rather than their age, who do not look upon gardening as a 'backyard' activity but more as a mild form of environmental activism. It is just this kind of thing which I was aiming to celebrate, promote and encourage with the formation of the volunteer-run Chelsea Fringe Festival, which is now in its fourth year, with more than three hundred events across three weeks in London and other cities.

The trend was even reflected at the Chelsea Flower Show this year, where the community-garden idea has largely superseded the ecologically correct garden as a favoured marketing tool for show-garden sponsors. Several of the extravaganzas on Main Avenue were billed as 'urban community gardens', notably those sponsored by Homebase and by Morgan Stanley. I did look slightly askance at this when I discovered how little these corporate sponsors are doing in the real world to foster actual community gardening.

Homebase was using its Chelsea 'community garden' chiefly to promote a new range of 'urban plants'. I suggested to its marketing department that they could perhaps foster some community gardening in the vicinity of their three hundred stores by issuing a discount card (twenty per cent off?) to local community gardens and by offering help and advice in kind. To its credit, Homebase have at least entered into a dialogue about this.

As for Morgan Stanley, it transpires that the full extent of its community-garden activity in the UK consists of the relocation of its frankly oligarchical Chelsea show garden to a housing estate in Poplar, near to the bank's offices in Canary Wharf. When I alluded to this shortcoming in print, I was within hours contacted by one of Morgan Stanley's public-relations executives, who told me that the bank's managing director wanted to see me in person at their Chelsea garden 'to explain why the firm is not, as you wrote "jumping on that [community] bandwagon for marketing purposes" with their Healthy Cities Garden'.

Who am I to disobey such a directive? I went along to the garden where it was explained to me that the garden was just one small part of a larger 'Healthy Cities' campaign. In turn I explained to the director that it seemed to me that one – completely inappropriate – Chelsea show garden reinstalled somehow in a housing estate in Poplar did not represent a contribution to community gardening that is proportionate to the resources Morgan Stanley has at its disposal. Why not a dozen, or twenty, community gardens or playgrounds across east London, as opposed to one repurposed marketing exercise?

The designer of the garden, Chris Beardshaw, explained that the idea was to transport the entire Chelsea garden (lupins, sculptures, water feature) to Poplar where it would be the 'the jewel, the centrepiece' of a new community garden. I suggested that it bore no resemblance whatsoever to any community garden I had ever seen and that in general what people want are productive spaces to grow fruit and veg, a pleasant and safe place to sit and relax, a convenient water source and good maintenance. The designer conceded that following some consultation with residents, vegetable beds were to be planted around the perimeter of his design.

The people of Poplar want and deserve the best, of course, but I'm not convinced that necessarily means a re-purposed Chelsea show garden. Subsequently I spoke to Babu Bhattacherjee of Harca Poplar, the housing organization which looks after the estate where the Morgan Stanley garden is going. He said that the expectation at their end was not for an exact copy of the Chelsea show garden but for 'a different design'. It emerged that the community, which is largely Bangladeshi, had indeed asked for a productive garden during the 'consultation', and that what they will be given instead is some raised beds adjacent to Chris Beardshaw's 'jewel'. For them, a proposed greenhouse and cooking space is the main beneficial addition to the site – though Bhattacherjee added that Morgan Stanley have not offered to fund this or other gardening activities.

During the course of our conversation at Chelsea, I was accused of being 'cynical' by the Morgan Stanley executive and of 'peddling negativity' by Chris Beardshaw. One does not want to seem negative or ungrateful towards companies which get involved in this way, but equally it can be argued that it is reasonable to expect their contribution in the real world to be proportionate to the marketing advantage they seek – bearing in mind that a Chelsea show garden is essentially a marketing exercise. Britain needs more of the feelgood factor of community gardening described so dramatically in *London Road*. So when it comes to sponsorship perhaps it is right to play Oliver Twist and say: 'Please, sir, I want some more.'

Daily Telegraph

THE EDUCATION OF A GARDENER
JULY 2015
↭

ON A BRIGHT MORNING early this month I find Luciano Giubbilei deep in a vegetable patch in Sussex, south-east England. This is not the kind of habitat with which the Italian garden designer is usually associated.

Born in Siena, he trained in London in the mid-1990s and has since based his highly successful practice there, creating gardens for clients in wealthy neighbourhoods such as Holland Park and Belgravia. His signature look is one of crisp perfection, his designs dignified by the green topiary forms in clipped box and hornbeam which one associates with Italian formal gardens, complemented by smooth lawns, perfectly still pools, elegant rills and smooth limestone terracing. It's garden design for the super-rich.

So what is he doing here, among the mud and radishes?

It has to be said that this is not just any old veg patch in any old garden. This is Great Dixter, the garden created by the cult plantsman Christopher Lloyd across more than half a century, where old topiary hedges barely contain some of the most exuberant and exciting plantings to be found anywhere. For the British – and also the French, Dutch and Germans, who take to the cross-Channel ferry in their droves to visit – the garden is a place of pilgrimage. Their veneration has if anything deepened after Lloyd's death in 2006, when head gardener Fergus Garrett took over, since he has proved to be quite as visionary as his late employer.

But Giubbilei is not here as a visitor: he is here to work. The object of his attention is a single flower bed, about ten metres long and three metres wide, at the far end of the vegetable garden, in a rather obscure corner where few visitors venture. It is neither labelled nor marked on the map of the garden, but that is how Giubbilei wants it to be – for this is his horticultural laboratory, a place where he can experiment with plants and learn more about their habits and virtues, and in so doing hone a new voice as a garden designer.

The question one might reasonably ask is: why? Giubbilei has been hugely successful commercially and also won the ultimate Best Show Garden award at last year's Chelsea Flower Show. But he is himself acutely aware that there has always been some feeling 'in the trade' that his work is stylish yet just a little safe, perhaps lacking some of the creative verve of British designers who turn to plants as their main mode of expression. I recall having dinner with him in Paris several years ago, when this matter came up in conversation, and it clearly rankled. He told me then that he felt he was at a crossroads in his career and was looking to change his 'voice' as a designer.

Giubbilei created that opportunity for himself in 2011, when he wrote to Fergus Garrett out of the blue, asking whether he could come to Great Dixter to learn more about plants. As Garrett recalls, 'I had never met him before and people were telling me that the last thing I needed was this guy in the garden – but I spoke to him on the phone and he seemed so nice, so genuine and so keen that I just knew it was the right thing to do.' For Giubbilei, it was a matter of addressing a gap in his knowledge. 'I grew up in the centre of town and we had no flowers,' he says. 'We had only geraniums on a windowsill. When I was a child, I don't remember ever seeing a garden with flowers.'

At this time he also had a pivotal conversation with the fashion designer Paul Smith. 'I met him at Chelsea and he invited me to his studio,' Giubbilei remembers. 'He showed me a lot of different ideas and books – like one on old Irish houses, where the paint was peeling off. And he said to me, "If this was the feel of a garden, how would you make it?" He said, "Your gardens are getting better, but now you should find a place to learn something, somewhere slower than your normal pace, where you can find a connection with what gardens are really about." He felt that for me the focus should be the atmosphere of a garden – that I should work on that, become more part of the process, go back to the soil.'

Giubbilei has certainly gone back to the soil at Great Dixter, where he now works two or three days a month on his border, assisted by one of the so-called student gardeners (who, under Garrett's inspired tutelage, tend to rise quickly to the top of the profession). This is a garden which is fine-tuned each and every day, where the aesthetics of planting have been taken to a new level. It is this creative atmosphere, and the relationship with Garrett, which Giubbilei finds most rewarding of all, even more than the hands-on horticulture.

'When I came here, I said to Fergus, "I am in a moment where I am facing a bit of a crisis." I had this book about my gardens which had been published, I had made these flower show gardens and I had a lot of clients, but my heart was pulling me in another direction. Fergus told me, "First, this is the perfect space for you. And if you want to learn something, you can work in this border rather than just follow me around. Secondly, design is very important. Because flowers without design . . . they are just flowers. So don't underestimate that."'

(For his part, Garrett tells me that Giubbilei has an exceptionally good eye and that his understanding of spatial design has translated into his treatment of plant masses. When I speak to him later, he recalls: 'I said to him, "Look, this isn't a photograph – it's not something you make for the moment. It's all about progression."')

'I am very ambitious,' Giubbilei continues. 'I want to learn and I want to learn from the best. Fergus has very little time – I had twenty minutes here at this table with him at six o'clock this morning. But that is an enriching moment for me. He talks to me very directly about what I should think about in terms of my own development. For me he is a total mentor. He has given me a new direction and the aim of being more ambitious with my designs.'

Giubbilei has also been drawn into the special working atmosphere created by Garrett at Great Dixter, where the head gardener takes on a role almost akin to that of a benign abbot presiding over a group of hard-working nuns and monks (the gardeners' on-site accommodation is fairly spartan). The parallel resonates with Giubbilei. 'There is something Zen about it,' he says. 'When you spend time here with Fergus and the gardeners and you see their attitude and how they are together, it is comforting. They have their routines, their breaks together, and they share these values. It's like a home. And it is now my home, too. I find it extremely comforting that I am welcome here.'

The question is, has his time in Sussex actually changed Giubbilei's work on the ground? His 2014 Chelsea show garden certainly had a new sense of authenticity in terms of the planting (devised at Great Dixter), and he says his professional design work has also changed. 'There is now much more plant material in my work, and also an expansion in scale,' Giubbilei explains. 'My gardens are more naturalistic. There is a simplicity to the layout still, but I want to have more of the sense of the place reflected in the content of the planting, wherever I am working in the world.

'Longevity through the seasons is what you need to understand. It's all to do with spacing and how you group the plants; it's all about patience. You have to understand the different moments of the season, and that plants might be there for one particular moment. You have to learn to wait.'

New York Times

RE-VITA-LIZING SISSINGHURST
SEPTEMBER 2015

↬

BACK IN 2008 I wrote an article suggesting that the garden at Sissinghurst Castle, in Kent, famously the creation of poet and garden-maker Victoria ('Vita') Sackville-West and her husband, the diplomat Harold Nicolson, had rather lost its mojo. It seemed to me that while it was being gardened at a high level, horticulturally speaking, the tone of the planting and general atmosphere of the place was a long way from anything Vita would have recognized. There was little of the romantic effusiveness, the pleasant disorder – at times shading into chaos – which this aristocratic owner, the very epitome of 'shabby chic', had carefully nurtured in her lifetime. Instead the garden was presented as a neat, well-organized and professionally run visitor attraction. It had lost its romance. Vita had vanished.

To my astonishment, this elicited a furious reaction from a former head of gardens at the National Trust. He fired off a 'green-ink letter' to the then director-general of the Trust, Dame Fiona Reynolds, stating that I was a discredit to the National Trust's gardens advisory panel.

Fortunately I was not sacked from this job (or should we say 'role', as it was voluntary). But I was taken aback by the force of feeling.

I shouldn't have been. Sissinghurst – more than any other garden I know – inspires extremes of emotion. There is a feeling that this is Britain's leading garden – and arguably therefore the world's – a status which has proven to be both a great boon and an albatross around its neck.

The truth is that the views I expressed then were not even particularly controversial; it's just that the relentlessly celebratory tone of most garden journalism meant that no one had actually said it in print. Many if not most people in the gardens world felt there was something wrong at Sissinghurst. A 2009 television series about Sissinghurst (made by my wife, as it happens) graphically demonstrated that the 'donor family' – led by Adam Nicolson and his wife Sarah Raven – felt the same way about the entire estate.

That has all changed. The fourth general manager in four years looks set to stay, and a new head gardener, Troy Scott Smith, has been appointed with the explicit mission to 're-Vita-lize' the garden. Judging by my last visit, in June, it appears that Sissinghurst is already well on the road to recovery. There is a new sense of fullness to key areas (notably the rose garden – because it is now understood that shrub roses are the key to the garden) as well as evidence of a new sensitivity to atmosphere and the importance of fine detail to this.

Scott Smith is the key to this success. He 'gets it'. As one member of the Nicolson family said (or rather demonstrated) to me, Vita would have thrown up her hands in dismay at the garden's former management; but she would be throwing her arms around Scott Smith today.

As a long-standing National Trust man, Scott Smith understands how the organization functions – which certainly helps. He was previously head gardener at Bodnant and before that at The Courts; crucially, early in his career he spent five years as a gardener at Sissinghurst. On visits back to the garden over the years, he admits: 'There was something which just bothered my about the place – the look and the feel of it. I was very content at Bodnant but when this job was advertised I thought about it and it became quite clear to me what was wrong. Sissinghurst should be really intimate and romantic and immersive. A soft wash should permeate the garden. But it had become too frigid, too processed. Beyond the garden, some parts were too municipal in feel. Before the interview I sent a paper to the Trust setting out where some of the faults lay and what could be done about them.'

To the Trust's credit, it accepted this critique and is supportive of Scott Smith's plan. Some of his proposed changes – such as plans to get rid of some of the hard paved paths and reinstate grass, or for the removal of too-smart column bases – might be apparent even to the casual visitor. But most of his interventions involve the texture and tone of the planting, which he says had become rather stale, with the same groupings – such as lupins in clumps of six – repeated year on year for decades and tactics such as individual plants like foxgloves placed to look as if they had self-seeded.

'The garden did not feel as if it was breathing and alive,' Scott Smith suggests. 'In Vita's day, hedges were cut to have character and the borders were full to overflowing.' Indeed, Vita's stated intention was to 'cram, cram, cram'.

The irony, as Scott Smith admits, is that the 'Vita way' does not come naturally to him. He is a professionally trained gardener who likes everything to be just so. He has sympathy with his predecessors, who were after all working to a high level in a style in which they had been trained and with the encouragement and approval of the higher-ups at the National Trust. It's more a case that the garden style at Sissinghurst was a reflection of the times: it became a garden of connoisseurial herbaceous-perennial horticulture in the style of Great Dixter or Beth Chatto's garden, high water marks in the 1980s and 1990s.

But Scott Smith says that this professional distance actually works to his and the garden's advantage, because Sissinghurst 'demands an intellectual as well as an intuitive approach – we have to be able to articulate what we are doing to the team and to the public.'

In support of this, I have a theory that an awful lot of female gardeners of a certain age subconsciously want to 'be' Vita Sackville-West. The idea plays on all kinds of fantasies, not least those bound up with social class. This is patently ridiculous for someone like Scott Smith (married with two children and sporting designer stubble). His professionalism arguably creates a stronger sense of focus.

There is much work still at be done at Sissinghurst. The opening salvo of the garden, the Top Courtyard, in particular, still exhibits a certain stiffness. But Scott Smith is clear that he is moving deliberately slowly and carefully, aware that you cannot rush a transformation such as this. Garden designer Dan Pearson is now working alongside Scott Smith as a consultant, visiting a few times a year and acting as a sounding board and collaborator. The proposed vision will emerge over a period of at least a decade, though already the changes are decisively affecting the atmosphere – for example, Scott Smith has already upped the rose content of the garden by 40 per cent, and there are many other explicit changes in the offing.

At risk of inspiring another green-ink letter, may I suggest that something of Vita is finally being brought back to Sissinghurst?

Daily Telegraph

CONNIE
OCTOBER 2015
꩜

CONSTANCE SPRY – 'Connie' to her friends – is known to posterity as the society florist par excellence, responsible for adorning shops, restaurants and churches with her boldly innovative arrangements. But towards the end of her life she expressed discontent with this reputation, since her instincts were democratic and her early career had been dedicated to helping the poorest in society.

In any case, Spry was a late starter. It was only in 1927, when she was forty-three and had been both divorced and an East End headmistress, that Spry was catapulted into the upper echelons of London society. Her first job, thanks to the interior designer Norman Wilkinson, was to 'do the flowers' for the window display of Atkinsons perfumery in the West End. In the 1930s Spry established herself as the leading 'floral decorator' (as she preferred to be known) in London, the toast of a coterie including Oliver Messel and Syrie Maugham, interior designers with whom she regularly collaborated. Society weddings followed, then ducal and royal commissions, and ultimately the Coronation of Elizabeth II in 1953, the crowning achievement of Spry's career, when she was put in charge of the cold banquet as well as the flowers.

Rarely can a life have been so utterly transformed, and with such alacrity.

Constance Fletcher was born on 5 December 1886 in a terrace house behind Derby railway station. Her father was a telegraphist with the Midland Railway Company who later became a schools inspector. The young Connie developed a liking for flowers early on, thanks to long country walks with a nursemaid. In 1900, when Connie was fourteen, the family moved to Dublin and she was sent to Alexandra College for Girls, which had a substantial garden. As a teenager, Connie took to arranging flowers at Dublin dinner parties – though she incurred her mother's displeasure on one occasion when she came up with a table display of rose petals in bowls of water in the dining room of a civic dignitary. Inspired by her father's public-spirited attitudes, at the age of nineteen Connie came to London to train as a health lecturer, with the intention of educating the poor about hygiene and nutrition.

Her career was curtailed in 1910 by an unsuitable and reportedly unconsummated marriage to a mine manager in Ireland. The Great War intervened, mercifully in this case, and by 1917 Connie was ready for divorce and a move back to London with her baby son. As Mrs Marr, after the war she took a position as the inspirational headmistress of a 'continuation school' in Homerton, East London, where she introduced carpentry and dressmaking, as well as plant identification. Her second 'husband' was Shav Spry, a civil servant – though in fact the pair were never legally married: a closely guarded secret.

After their move to an Essex farmhouse in 1925, Spry made a garden and also began to create flower arrangements on a commercial basis for weddings and parties. Her life suddenly changed in 1927 when she met Norman Wilkinson at a London luncheon and was invited to design the flowers for Atkinsons, as well as arrangements for the foyers of a chain of London cinemas, Spry promptly resigned her teaching post and – to her family's consternation – left the world of good works for a vivacious career in flowers and fine food.

Though she was not a glamorous or beautiful person, nor even particularly stylish in dress (she preferred working clothes), Spry was accepted into the world of interior design, theatre and fashion, dominated by homosexual men. After all, she was an outsider, too. For this rather dowdy but eminently sparky and creative erstwhile headmistress, who boasted not a cut-glass accent but a pleasant melange of Dublin and Derbyshire, this represented an *entrée* into high society. The garden writer Beverley Nichols became a firm friend, as did the actor John Gielgud, whose sister came to work at Spry's first shop, which opened in Pimlico in 1931 (then a rather unfashionable locale).

As for her designs, Spry became known early on for her use of humble plant material and hedgerow flowers, such as willowherb, giant fennel, elderberry and cow parsley, and for her liking for simple but dramatic displays on green-and-white themes. Her whole approach to flower design was geared to authentic self-expression (not 'fashion') and an attempt to create arrangements which were suited both to the room and to the occasion for which they were designed. It was this simple idea – allied with her natural genius for composition – which raised Spry's work far above traditional floristry practice, which seemed stiff and boring by comparison.

She also sought to create a distinction between her approach and that of great gardeners such as Gertrude Jekyll and Maria Theresa Earle. In her first book, *Flower Decoration* (1934), Spry stated: 'Then there are books by eminent gardeners whose knowledge and love of flowers is so great that their views command respect, but it is natural that they should treat the subject from the point of view of displaying flowers rather than of decorating rooms.'

In the early 1930s Syrie Maugham's celebrated luncheons became the vehicle for Spry's most fantastical and imaginative floral creations, many of them in the pure-white style associated with the interior designer, then at the height of popularity in society. Huge lilies and hydrangeas became a signature look. Spry also began to design flowers for Heal's department store, though it later transpired that she had negotiated a fee of just a pound a week for her services. This wholly unrealistic figure was typical for Spry, who was never a good businesswoman. For accounting, she came to depend on a close female colleague who worked alongside her husband and pursued a long-term affair with him – apparently with Spry's knowledge. For her part, the newly emancipated Spry embarked on a relationship with Hannah Gluckstein, known as 'Gluck', a mercurial Hampstead artist who liked to dress in men's suits.

Ever more successful as the decade progressed, Spry relocated to larger premises in Burlington Gardens before opening a shop at 64 South Audley Street, as well as the Constance Spry Flower School in a basement in Curzon Street, Mayfair. Flower decoration had become an acceptable pastime (or way of passing the time) for young unmarried women – as had cookery: Spry's flower school would eventually merge with the Cordon Bleu Cookery School, run by her friend Rosemary Hume.

The regimen for the young ladies in Spry's employ was always to call at the front door of clients' residences (never the tradesmen's entrance) and always to create their arrangements in situ in the rooms in which they were destined to stand, as opposed to in the scullery or pantry. The floral decorators' uniform consisted of a hat and pink overalls. The flowers were mainly sourced from the London markets, or from the garden of Spry's home (she had a succession of houses), though Spry would also walk in clients' gardens and pick flowers destined for the arrangements. She was always careful not to overfill vases; indeed, the receptacle – whether glass, china, brass or stone – was generally treated as no less important than the plants.

There was occasional confusion as to the social status of the visiting team from Flower Decorations Ltd. One chatelaine who had treated Spry and her colleagues with hauteur before a party was reportedly mortified by the display of warm familiarity and admiration shown towards them when her guests arrived.

It was weddings which became the mainstay of the business in the 1930s. Constance Spry arrangements became almost de rigueur at society weddings. In 1935 Spry 'did the flowers' for the February wedding of Edwin Lutyens's daughter at St Margaret's, Westminster: huge branches of *Eucalyptus globulus*, the Tasmanian blue gum, the undersides of their leaves painted blue, arranged in urns to look like a waterfall. Spry's preferred approach in churches was for two huge displays at the chancel, with the rest of the church left alone. (As was the case with her floral predecessor Gertrude Jekyll, Spry used plants to complement architecture, not compete with it.) In St Paul's Cathedral she used huge phormium leaves with scarlet amaryllis flowers, to simple and dramatic effect. At another society wedding the bride carried a bouquet of blue gentians while Southwark Cathedral was adorned with twelve-foot-high displays of lilies, pampas grass and green hydrangeas (the last a very 'Spry' plant).

For the winter wedding of Nancy Beaton (Cecil's sister), Spry had the bridesmaids linked together with whitewashed ropes entwined with white flowers – fondly remembered by the family despite the fact that in the heated church interior the paint dripped off the ropes and left a long white trail down the aisle. Spry's most celebrated floral wedding display was for Lady Violet Bonham Carter, where she used humble cow parsley alone, in great masses in huge white urns. She repeated the look for a debutantes' ball at Claridge's.

All this was met with rapturous delight by the press in England and in America (where Spry opened a short-lived boutique in 1938). Spry's novel ideas about flower arrangements including vegetables, however, were met with hilarity in some quarters – at one public dinner a pile of Brussels sprouts was heaped before her and she was jokingly asked to create a display out of them. For once, Spry was lost for words.

Like many others in the world of gardens, Spry firmly believed in the power of flowers to raise the spirits at the bleakest times. From 1941, when she was invited by the Ministry of Information to lecture nationwide to female factory workers and military personnel, she encouraged war-weary women to create floral decorations. At this time she made a point of planning arrangements using only plants found on bombsites, and talked lyrically of the beauty of old English flowers – especially the old shrub roses which she championed alongside the likes of Vita Sackville-West and her friend Graham Stuart Thomas. In this spirit and to universal delight, Spry decorated the exterior of Coolings Art Gallery on Bond Street with huge displays of flowers and imitation grass lain across the sandbags.

It was during the war that Spry began to communicate her love for cooking: in 1942 she published her first cookbook, *Come into the Garden, Cook*, though she was to be best known in culinary circles for the fat cookbook bearing her name that was published in the next decade, seen as the successor to Mrs Beeton's book which dominated the previous century.

In the post-war years Spry was an early supporter of the craze for flower-arranging clubs and societies, though she disliked the emphasis on competition which developed, preferring to see the practice as an opportunity for freedom of expression. 'Study the growing plant,' she enjoined. 'Learn in the garden rather than in the floral art class.' At packed public meetings she would often be asked how to decorate a church, to which she would respond: 'What church, for what occasion, and with what flowers?'

The apogee of Spry's career was the invitation to decorate Westminster Abbey for the Coronation of Queen Elizabeth II. Thousands of red roses and other flowers were grown by the Royal Parks (the Superintendent of Parks collapsed and died of a heart attack on the eve of the Coronation) and many more were imported from foreign climes. The scale of the occasion and the sumptuousness required did not quite play to Spry's strengths, perhaps, and in the event it is the food she created for the occasion that is best remembered – notably her recipe for curried Coronation Chicken, which was served cold with cucumber rice. (The original nineteenth-century recipe which inspired it included dried apricots, but these were omitted by Spry.)

Spry's flower and cookery school was by this time ensconced in Winkfield Park, near Ascot, which she ran with close attention from a tiny flat on the premises. The young ladies attending the school were housed in bedrooms, not dormitories, as per Spry's stern stipulation. And it was here that she died suddenly one evening in 1960, to be mourned by an extremely wide circle of friends and acquaintances – very few of whom knew her very well at all, it appears.

Country Life

'CAPABILITY' BROWN
JANUARY 2016
↦

THIS YEAR sees the 300th anniversary of the birth of Lancelot Brown, the celebrated landscape designer whose nickname derived from his habit of remarking upon the 'capabilities' or potential of a landscape. To commemorate the year, dozens of landscape gardens associated with the name of 'Capability' Brown are opening up to the public (if they are in private hands) or else hosting special events such as walks and talks. He is after all the most celebrated landscape designer Britain has ever produced, with only André Le Nôtre of Versailles vying with him in terms of international fame.

So what is it that makes Capability Brown so special?

First, there is the sheer scale of his achievement. From the start of his career, as head gardener at Stowe in the 1740s, until his death in 1783, Brown advised or worked on at least 170 English estates (the exact number ebbs and flows according to documentary evidence). He exerted almost a monopoly on landscape style in the later eighteenth century, with aristocrats and landed gentry of all political stripes calling on his advice. (He was once asked why he had not created any landscape gardens in Ireland; his reply was that he had not yet finished England.) The political aspect is important because in the first half of the eighteenth century landowners of Tory or Whig persuasion had used landscape design as a way of expressing their political ideals or intellectual interests, often in a highly individualistic manner (as at Stowe). What Brown offered by contrast was a benignly apolitical vision which nevertheless incorporated elements of the formal classical vocabulary, such as temples, seats, Palladian bridges and porticoes – all shorn of the symbolic meaning with which they were previously freighted.

The 'Brown look', of rolling pasture right up to the house walls, decorous clumps or belts of trees, carefully sited lakes and false rivers (often with an attractive bridge or two), and entrance drives engineered for dramatic effect, became de rigueur in country houses of the day. Great estates such as Chatsworth, Bowood, Alnwick and Stowe were subject to a Brownian 'makeover'. Blenheim is perhaps his most celebrated work today, while Croome Court in Worcestershire (his first major commission) is currently the subject of an ambitious restoration by the National Trust.

In Brown's day vast sums could be expended on these projects, especially where substantial water features were planned, and as a result he became a very rich man indeed, also enjoying royal patronage later in his career, as master gardener at Hampton Court and High Sheriff of Huntingdonshire. Yet he never let up, covering huge distances on horseback even late in life, visiting far-flung estates and dispensing advice, charming clients and checking on the work of an army of gardeners and foremen (the average scheme took five years to complete). Even then, he could not be everywhere at once and mistakes did happen. As he wrote by way of apology to one disgruntled Wiltshire client: 'When I am galloping in one part of the world my men are making blunders and neglects.'

In rather a modern way, Brown engineered his own image as carefully as his landscapes. He was always careful to cultivate the appearance of a reliable yeoman who would not get above himself – plainly dressed in a brown coat in his portraits, like a country parson, and never publishing a word about his design precepts.

Despite his astonishing success, Brown has proved a controversial figure in garden history. The creation of his pastoral idylls in many cases led to the removal of the elaborate formal parterre gardens of the seventeenth century, and as a result he has been blamed for the virtual erasure of a key period in English landscape history. Recently Brown's sensitivity to existing formal landscapes has been more appreciated – he frequently retained formal features such as avenues of trees and straight carriage rides, just so long as the essential pastoralism of the scene was not undermined.

Another under-appreciated aspect of Brown's work is the sheer practicality of his landscape design in an estate setting. Those rolling acres of pasture near the house were conceived as haymaking factories, a vital resource on estates which relied on horsepower, while the clumps and belts of trees which fringed the park were also useful coverts for game birds, at a time when innovations in gun design led to game shooting becoming a mania among landowners. Even the artifical lakes Brown created doubled as stores of fish, waterfowl and otters for sport (despicable as that may seem today).

The great paradox of Brown's work, and the reason it is sometimes described as 'invisible', is that the whole point was to create an illusion of natural English countryside – and many of us over the centuries have fallen for it. Brown's achievements are all too easy to take for granted because we assume his landscapes have always been there. Yet a typical Brownian landscape is highly artificial, the result of earth moving, extensive tree planting (and removal), the erasure of buildings or even whole villages, and the creation or finessing of rivers and lakes. In a Brownian landscape, even the directions in which we look will be manipulated by the designer, by means of the placement of trees and hills. Brown eschewed vistas which ran straight out from the front of the house, for example, preferring diagonal sightlines from park to house and vice versa (preferably involving a change of level), and he would carefully organize numerous other cross vistas throughout the estate. Groups of trees were placed as 'staging posts' in a long vista, a technique which owed something to the composition of Claude Lorrain's landscape paintings, which were highly influential at the time (often hanging in the drawing rooms from which these very vistas could be espied). So despite the ostensible naturalism, the approach was rational and geometric: a plan view of the vistas on a typical Brown landscape design resembles something a contemporary computer programme might come up with.

Finally, it is worth celebrating the sheer versatility and flexibility of Capability Brown's design model. This was not a style which was simply 'rolled out' across England like a lorryload of turf. Each and every Brown landscape has its own distinctive features and bears the hand of the master, always working in tandem with the particularities of the landscape and its atmosphere – what the great eighteenth-century poet and gardener Alexander Pope called, 'the genius of the place'. Perhaps that is a fitting description, too, for Lancelot Brown.

House & Garden

WHERE IS THE BRITISH ART?
APRIL 2016

THE EXHIBITION now running at the Royal Academy – Monet to Matisse: Painting the Modern Garden – is not to be missed, but I have a nagging feeling of doubt about it. Something is missing, and that something is British art.

This is an art-historical observation rather than a patriotic objection. But it does seem a little strange that our own Royal Academy should foster a vision of an artistic period that entirely excludes paintings by Britons of our great national artform, garden-making.

Perhaps one clue to this curious omission is the fact that the exhibtion has been staged in partnership with an American institution (the Cleveland Museum of Art). The show appears to be predicated on an outdated but engrained 'beaux-arts' attitude to European art which was once summed up by the American intellectual Gertrude Stein with the dictum: 'Painting in the nineteenth century was only done in France and by Frenchmen'.

In fact there are just two canvases by British artists in the exhibition – one a forgettable effort by Alfred Parsons, and the other William Nicholson's much-reproduced study of Gertrude Jekyll's boots, which seems a little out of place given that it is not a painting of a garden.

This is hardly an adequate representation of British garden painting of the period. What of Stanley Spencer and Cedric Morris? Or John Nash and Ivon Hitchens? These artists made wonderfully intimate and acutely observed studies of gardens and plants. The RA show is also rather thin on female artists (only Berthe Morisot features), when it could have included the work of neglected women painters like Frances Hodgkins and Winifred Nicholson.

No one could argue that any of the paintings by Monet, Pissarro, Kandinsky or Klee should be dropped in favour of the work of British artists of the era. But on the other hand the RA exhibition contains numerous works by lesser known artists – including Joaquin Trinxet, Childe Hassam, Maurice Denis, Henri Le Sidaner and Santiago Rusinol – whose work could hardly be said to eclipse that of every single British artist of the late nineteenth and early twentieth century.

A room (or half a room?) of British work would have made for such an interesting counterpoint. As the painter Michael Ayrton observed, the British genius is founded upon 'the lyrical, the satiric, the mystical, the romantic, and the preoccupation with linear rhythms'. All of those qualities, except the satiric, can be found in British garden painting of this period (and the satiric, even, comes in the work of Edward Bawden and Eric Ravilious).

I would like to make a positive case for the dozen British artists working in the first half of the twentieth century who might be included in this putative Salon des Refusés. (There could have been several dozen more.)

First there is Stanley Spencer, who is arguably the greatest of all modern British painters of gardens and flowers. Over four decades he consecrated through painting his home village of Cookham in Berkshire; indeed it has been said that he 'made Cookham into a holy suburb of heaven', with flowers playing the part of angels and humble village front gardens taking on an intense air of symbolic meaning – as with the extraordinary Cottages at Burghclere (1927–31), where the painter seems to feel a moral obligation to render every particle of existence in the scene.

David Jones is another artist with an intense mystical vision. His painting *The Garden Enclosed* (1924), with its biblical overtones and panicky structure, is surely worthy to hang alongside the work of Paul Klee, the RA-approved artist whose work perhaps has most kinship with the British vision.

From an earlier generation, Walter Sickert's reputation has risen in recent years, despite his reputation for 'drabness'. If the work of Monet and the Impressionists is redolent of a summer holiday in warm climes, filled with luminescent colour, then Sickert's represents a depressingly dank British Monday when one returns to work – all greys and browns. But that is the point. In his paintings of unkempt London back gardens seen from his own humble digs, Sickert wanted to show life as it is. The power of his work lies in its structural invention and the extraordinary quality of atmosphere he is able to gather up.

Quite diffferent in style is the sumptuous painting of E.A. Hornel, a Scottish artist who made a notable garden at Broughton House, Kirkcudbright, which is open to the public today. Hornel's reputation rests on a series of forty-four richly coloured and textured paintings he made while on year-long trip to Japan in 1893. Many of them are garden scenes that depict kimono-clad women walking or dancing, as if they are themselves elements of the garden.

The work of Frances Hodgkins is being rediscovered in her native New Zealand but is almost forgotten in her adoptive country of Britain – hers was an uncompromising vision which ventured into the territory of symbolism in works such as *Sabrina's Garden* (1932). One of her best works, it paradoxically came out of a disastrous painting trip to Norfolk, which she found otherwise, à la Noel Coward, 'a depressing waste . . . & flat flat landscape – a lifeless outlook'.

Charles Mahoney is another artist whose work tended towards the mythic or symbolic – obviously in works such as *Adam and Eve in the Garden* (1932), which manages to make an English garden look like the equatorial jungle, and more subtly with superficially prosaic themes such as *Outhouses* (1940), where trees and buildings seem to coalesce into the texture of a vacant afternoon.

Several artists who are known as 'landscape painters' were in fact just as intrigued by the artificially enclosed setting of the garden, with all its theatricality and emotional intensity. (John Piper was one, but is outside our time frame.) John Nash quietly went on painting garden scenes while his brother Paul carved out a greater reputation, but his work is now almost as appreciated. He was able to capture that feeling of being perfectly alone in a garden, which can be quite a melancholic experience. Nash certainly knew his plants and latterly taught botanical illustration, noting that, 'the open innocent countenance of a daisy or anemone may seem easy to draw, but they too can prove to be a snare, and sometimes I prefer the hooded Labiates, helmeted Monkshood and Balsam, or the leering countenance of Foxglove and Penstemon.'

Ivon Hitchens is another indisputably important artist whose work might have found a place in the RA's galleries. He instinctively understood that certain aspects of the character of a garden or landscape will remain elusive or mysterious. His wide canvases, such as *Garden Cove* (1948), reflect the musical qualities of gardens and woodland. He once commented, 'I am always fascinated by the space left between the verticals of trees . . . These divide up the area into separate movements.' At the same time Hitchens revelled in the earthy fecundity of the garden scene, with all its unexpected writhings and sudden bright colorations.

Winifred Nicholson specialized in a fusion of still life and landscape, with bowls and vases poised on flower-festooned windowsills – her paintings are on one level decorative, but they also exude emotion and a sense of meaning.

Another painter who took flowers and gardens as a principal subject was Cedric Morris. His vision of flowers is sumptuous and celebratory, especially of his beloved irises. *Iris Seedlings* (1943) has something of the fraught dignity of the High Baroque. And Morris was, of course, a considerable gardener in his own right.

Laura Knight ought to be included for her great depiction of *Spring in St John's Wood* (1933), which is like doing up a top button and going outside into the stiffening breeze and half-forgotten sunshine. As an artistic migrant to Cornwall, she painted several other crisp depictions of women in sunlit gardens, many of them harbouring a distinct erotic undertone.

Finally, a wild card. Paul Maitland is a little-known painter whose studies of Kensington Gardens made in the 1890s are bursting with the remarkable, quietly immanent atmosphere such places often have. Maitland was a hunchback who lived reclusively and died in his mid forties. But he exhibitied with Sickert and I suspect that a garden audience, in particular, would appreciate his sensibility.

Perhaps the Royal Academy will be able to redress the imbalance of its current show at some point in the future. In the meantime, do go to the current exhibition if you can. All cavils aside, it is a marvellously escapist experience – yes, like a holiday away from these shores.

Daily Telegraph

IS YOUR GARDEN GOOD FOR YOU?
JULY 2016

IS YOUR GARDEN GOOD FOR YOU? Most of us would agree that it helps somewhat with physical fitness, though it's hardly a substitute for twenty squat-thrusts. Fresh air is supposed to be beneficial, and even a little light deadheading is presumably good for the circulation. But there are plenty of fat gardeners out there (and long may they continue to enjoy life).

What about mental health? That concept is all the rage at the moment. The National Gardens Scheme has just released a report they commissioned from The King's Fund about the beneficial effects of gardening on the mind, while the British Medical Association organized a series of events around the subject as part of this year's Chelsea Fringe Festival. The RHS is also pursuing the theme, having recently called for gardening to be prescribed on the National Health Service.

Needless to say, gardening comes out strongly in surveys regarding health benefits. All kinds of groups – ex-servicemen, disaffected youth, grieving widowers, recovering addicts – have demonstrated 'improved outcomes' as a result of gardening. In fact, gardening ticks so many boxes when it comes to measurable health benefits that it is likely to help the cause of community gardens and all sorts of other horticultural projects as they try to secure funding in the future (especially now that the useless Garden Bridge has gobbled up all the money).

So what's not to like about the idea of gardens and health? Well, I don't want to undermine any of these good works in any way, but a little part of me does worry that the mantra that 'gardening is good for you' encourages the condescending caricature that horticulture is only fit for damaged people who require help and succour. That role is not to be scoffed at, but surely it's more complicated than that? If we want more young people to enter the horticultural profession, perhaps we ought to be careful not to narrow its appeal by portraying it as primarily a branch of occupational therapy.

In the interests of balance, it may be worth thinking about some of the more challenging aspects of gardening.

Take physical health. At this time of year I spend a lot of time visiting gardens, and in the past few weeks I have seen someone fall off a brick wall straight into a flowerbed while watering (hilarious), and another person tumble into a small pond while trying to forage a wild herb (even more hilarious – they were just a little bit too pleased with themselves for their knowledge of wild herbs).

Of course one should not really jest about this topic, because serious accidents can occur in the garden. The most recent data available from the Royal Society for the Prevention of Accidents indicates that lawnmowers account for most garden accidents – an estimated 6,500 each year – while secateurs come in as the third most dangerous garden item, the cause of some 4,400 accidents. Perhaps that is no surprise. But what about the second biggest cause of accidents in gardens – can you guess? It is salutary to learn that the cause of an estimated 5,300 accidents was the humble flowerpot. (Lifting injuries and trips are the culprits.)

As for mental health, gardening can surely be quite challenging at times. Is it taboo to suggest that a garden can make you feel bad, sometimes, as well as good? I have come to look upon domestic gardens in terms of relationships above all and, as with human affairs, these do not always run smooth. Many people have an intense daily relationship with their garden – in some cases more intense than with their spouse or partner. They might, at different times, feel ecstatic affection or near-hatred for it. They may even end up divorcing their garden – by moving house.

Gardens induce complex and nuanced relationships which cannot simply be reduced to blandishments about health benefits. People who are using gardening for rehabilitative purposes are of course just as likely as anyone else to experience a deep sense of connection with the natural world, or to form a 'relationship'. My concern is the status of gardening in the wider culture. It must be understood that we do not garden chiefly because it is good for us. Gardening and gardens are dynamic, powerful and profound, not benignly passive. It is their richness and unpredictability, the ways they constantly surprise, delight – and occasionally disappoint or infuriate – that keep us coming back for more.

Daily Telegraph, Medlar column

INDEX

ACKNOWLEDGMENTS

I would like to thank my editor at Pimpernel Press, Jo Christian, for suggesting the book and seeing it to press with customary aplomb. Gail Lynch proffered wise counsel. I am fortunate enough to have two designers: Becky Clarke has created a fun jacket, while Anne Wilson has laid out the text elegantly. The dedication to this book is a little jokey but in seriousness I would like to thank all the magazine and newspaper editors who have valued my work and commissioned me to write over the years. Too many to name here – you know who you are!

Special thanks are owed to the following publications, for their kind permission to reprint here articles which first appeared in their pages.

Country Life
My week   May 2007
American alligators   January 2009
Ghosts   January 2010
Chanticleer meets Great Dixter   May 2010
Fifth season   September 2011
Connie   October 2015

Daily Telegraph
Great Dixter   May 2009
Rosemary Verey   November 2010
Lost heroes of gardening   December 2010
Cycling to gardens   January 2011
Natural playspace   September 2011
Yellow Book   March 2012
Rodmarton   June 2012
Bekonscot model village   September 2012
The resonant ash   November 2012
Korea   August 2013
Night gardens   October 2013
Jellicoe at Runnymede   November 2013
Haunted garden   December 2014
Alice   February 2015
A Little Chaos   March 2015
On islands   April 2015
From Versailles to Poplar   May 2015
Re-Vita-lizing Sissinghurst   September 2015
Where is the British art?   April 2016
Is your garden good for you?   July 2016

Evening Standard
Chelsea Flower Show   May 2015

Financial Times
Landform   First published in the *Financial Times How to Spend It* magazine in April 2010
Tree planting   First published in the *Financial Times How to Spend It* magazine in January 2012
Shrubs make a comeback   First published in the *Financial Times How to Spend It* magazine in October 2014

Gardens Illustrated
Tom Stuart-Smith   July 2007
Mikinori Ogisu   August 2007
Sissinghurst again   January 2008
Duisburg Nord   November 2008
Villa Gamberaia   March 2009
Serre de la Madone   January 2010
Robin Lane Fox in Oxford   September 2010
Long Barn   May 2015

House & Garden
'Capability' Brown   January 2016

The Idler
The politics of self-sufficiency   December 2009

Literary Review
Ian Hamilton Finlay   April 2009
Museum Without Walls   November 2013

New York Times
The education of a gardener   July 2015

Sunday Times
Piet Oudolf in Somerset   August 2014